The Student Mindset

A 30-item toolkit for anyone learning anything

Steve Oakes and Martin Griffin

Crown House Publishing Limited
www.crownhouse.co.uk

First published by

Crown House Publishing Ltd
Crown Buildings, Bancyfelin, Carmarthen, Wales, SA33 5ND, UK
www.crownhouse.co.uk

and

Crown House Publishing Company LLC
PO Box 2223, Williston, VT 05495, USA
www.crownhousepublishing.com

British Library of Cataloguing-in-Publication Data

A catalogue entry for this book is available from the British Library.

Print ISBN 978-178583308-3
Mobi ISBN 978-178583392-2
ePub ISBN 978-178583393-9
ePDF ISBN 978-178583394-6

LCCN 2018961109

Printed and bound in the UK by Gomer Press, Llandysul, Ceredigion

Contents

Acknowledgements

Thanks to all at Crown House Publishing who encouraged us as we worked on this project. Many thanks in particular to those who've helped us shape the book: David and Karen Bowman for their thoughtful feedback and consistent support; Daniel Bowen for his assistance; Beverley Randell and Rosalie Williams for all their hard work; and Emma Tuck for her attention to detail. Graphics and design have been important on this project so a big thank you goes to Tom Fitton for his tremendous work.

Manchester Metropolitan University has been an important part of this project – thanks for the debate and discussion, non-stop coffee and endless snacks. Special thanks go to Dr Jennifer McGahan for her relentless support of the VESPA model and for making sure that we stay research-informed.

We would also like to thank Kevin Green at the Manchester Health Academy and all his staff for testing and trying the VESPA tools with their students. And, of course, special thanks to our families for everything else.

Visit us at thestudentmindset.com, follow us on Twitter @vespamindset for our latest updates or say hello via thestudentmindset@gmail.com.

Introduction

We've spent a combined forty years studying how people learn.

We've followed students who battle through difficult times, stay positive and get really good results – and wished we could be the same. We've worked with students who get exasperated, unfocused and demotivated – and recognised our past selves in them too.

We've spoken to thousands of students about how they study and what they do every day or week that makes a difference. We've discussed the problems we all face when we try to learn something new.

We've discovered huge amounts.

For example, we've learned that past success does not correlate with future success; some students with a track record of underperforming go on to achieve amazing results, while others with a great track record don't achieve what they were hoping for.

We've seen scores of students persist with approaches that aren't working well and spoken to hundreds of students who have decided to study in new ways. Many of the latter have seen their results change significantly as they've adjusted their tactics. We've seen that while cognitive factors can be important, non-cognitive factors also play a huge role in academic success.

Most importantly, we've found that there are a set of tools and strategies that keep coming up when we ask successful students what it is they do. They seem to be in control – they're balanced, grounded and happy despite the challenges of study.

We've been lucky enough to borrow these techniques and apply them to our own studies. We're both currently students ourselves, and we've become better learners by stealing the tricks and tactics associated with calm, purposeful study and, ultimately, getting good results.

In short, we've discovered that academic success isn't just about intelligence. This might seem counterintuitive at first, but time after time we've seen students do well because of the way they work – the routines, strategies and habits they've created for themselves.

These tricks and tactics are what this book is all about.

VESPA

So what are the tools and techniques used by successful learners? We've become so obsessed that we've begun collecting them, reading about them and practising them. We've started designing our own and testing them with students.

For us, it's become clear that these strategies sit in one of five groups, each associated with a particular characteristic. The five characteristics or qualities we've discovered in high performing students are vision, effort, systems, practice and attitude, or VESPA.

Let's take them one at a time ...

Vision

> *Mindset starts with ambition because our potential is limited by our ambition. High aspirations drive us to take more risk, have more courage, show more resilience and be more positive.*

Owen (2015), p. 17

Figuring out *why* you're studying helps to release extra levels of commitment, determination and positivity. When times are tough, high vision students can remember why they're going through difficulties. They persist for longer and manage to remain optimistic. And so students with a strong vision get better results. So:

- Do you have a clear plan for the future?
- Have you written down your goals?

Vision is about having a well-defined goal: it's about making a connection between the work you are doing and your reason for doing it. In simple terms it's about knowing the outcomes you want to achieve and developing an appetite to achieve them. Angela Duckworth, the distinguished professor of psychology at the University of Pennsylvania, calls this 'grit'. In her book of the same name, Duckworth (2016) found that people who know clearly what they want to achieve, and then stick to it, are more likely to be successful. They're more gritty.

How might you measure a person's grit? Duckworth and her team developed an interesting questionnaire that you might want to try yourself – here's the link: https://angeladuckworth.com/grit-scale/.

If you complete the questionnaire, don't worry if your score seems low. You might not have had the opportunity to fully develop your grit yet. It might be worth spending some time thinking about when you've been most gritty. What were you doing? At what stage of your life? Finally, and most importantly, how are you going to be gritty when you're studying?

If we dig deep enough, most of us have a vision – a big goal we'd like to achieve. It's important not to let people talk you out of your goal or tell you that you can't do it. Distance yourself from those who do. One of the best ways to get clarity on your goals is to write them down and reflect on them.

There are seven vision activities in this book. If you want to jump in and do all of them, they're on pages 18, 35, 38, 42, 46, 48 and 116.

Effort

> *I believe that my success is due in part to some level of skill. But more than that, I believe that I win because I out-work people.*

Gary Vaynerchuk (quoted in Brock, 2016)

We've asked thousands of students how hard they work, and then checked this against the results they achieve. The students with the best results work harder than the others. But when we spoke to low effort students, they thought they were working hard too. *Perceptions of effort are personal and relative*. So:

- When was the last time you worked really hard on something? What were you doing?
- Have you ever worked so hard on something that time just flew by?

The effort element of the model refers to how much work you do. Pretty much anything worth achieving requires effort. You might be aware of the 10,000 hour rule suggested by K. Anders Ericsson (2016). His research found that most experts have dedicated over 10,000 hours to their craft to become an 'expert', a fact popularised by Malcolm Gladwell in his book *Outliers: The Story of Success* (2008).

A quick internet search will reveal many students who claim to have studied with minimum effort – the PhD completed in 100 days or the master's dissertation written in a weekend. We wouldn't recommend that you use these as your benchmark. People are always looking for short cuts, but most students who achieve good results will have worked hard. It's as simple as that.

Don't panic though! We're not discussing a vast and endless 10,000 hours of nose-to-the-grindstone effort here. Effort varies from field to field. And while there isn't much research out there giving us a clear answer on exactly how much effort is needed to pass particular qualifications at certain levels or ages, what is clear to us is that high levels of effort are a habit. And anyone can start a new habit.

There are five effort activities in this book. If you want to race through all of them, they're on pages 77, 122, 133, 136 and 141.

Systems

Creativity x Organization = Impact

Belsky (2010), p. 27

Being organised allows you to collect and collate learning material and then see the connections between topics and ideas, which allows you to understand material more quickly. Organising your day well means that you get more done in less time. These two tricks – one to do with resources and the other to do with time – are at the heart of why high systems students get better results. So:

- What does your study area look like? Is it tidy or messy? What about your files and folders?
- Do you stick to deadlines? Are you measured and methodical, or always in crisis mode?

System is about two things: (1) organising your learning and (2) organising your time. Students often overlook the importance of being organised. There's been some interesting research which suggests that struggling with particular academic challenges is more to do with a lack of organisation than a lack of intellectual ability. Most students will have to deal with the battles of time management, procrastination and systematising information.

We've found that students get a significant return on their investment if they develop their systems, and over the years we've picked up some great tools to help you.

There are five systems activities in this book. If you want to skip ahead and do them all, they're on pages 56, 59, 63, 66 and 70.

Practice

> *For the things we have to learn before we can do them, we learn by doing them.*

Aristotle, *The Nicomachean Ethics*, p. 23

Learning isn't memorising information. It's memorising information and then using it to achieve certain things – to construct an argument, solve a problem, interpret unfamiliar data, build something new. High practice students get good results because they spend time practising using their information flexibly and creatively to achieve an objective. Low practice students stop once they've memorised their information (or they stop *before* they've finished memorising it!). So:

- When was the last time you tested yourself?
- How would you advise someone to revise for an exam?

We see practice as distinct from effort – it represents what learners do with their studies. It's the *how* of studying. When it comes to learning quickly, it's the way you practise that counts. It's hard to talk about practice without mentioning the work of K. Anders Ericsson, mentioned earlier. He has spent his entire career looking at top level performers in a number of fields. His conclusion is that top performers don't just practise hard, they *practise in a particular way*.

There are four practice activities in the book. If you want to complete them all at once, they're on pages 80, 83, 92 and 97.

Attitude

> *Students who are success seekers are not bluffed by setback, poor performance, failure or academic adversity. They take the lesson to be learnt and move on. They do not dwell on the mistake; they learn from it. They do not conclude they are dumb or no good; they see mistakes and setbacks as reflecting on their effort, attitude, or the way they went about the task, which all can be improved next time. They do not assume that past failure will predict future failure.*

Martin (2010), p. 22

Everyone goes through difficulties when learning. For some of the students we've talked to, these difficulties are evidence that they're not good enough. Many of them withdraw their effort, retreat from challenges, and eventually give up. The high attitude students we've interviewed and observed know that difficulties are to be expected. They keep going when times are tough, and get better results because of this. So:

- How do you respond when something goes wrong?
- How do you learn from your mistakes?

We all know how important having the right attitude is; it's quite often what separates performance in any field. For students to be successful we think you need four aspects of attitude. First, you need confidence in your abilities - confidence is key to academic success. Second, you need to be able to control your emotions in high stakes situations. Third, you need to respond positively when feedback indicates there is still a lot of work to be done to improve. Finally, you need a growth mindset. This means that you have to believe that you *can* improve.

We've spoken to hundreds of students who appear to have this positive attitude in their DNA. But in fact they've just developed, sometimes subconsciously, a series of tricks and techniques to get themselves through challenging periods. We're going to share some of these with you.

Attitude is key, so there are nine attitude activities in this book. If you want to push on and do all of them at once, they're on pages 23, 27, 50, 86, 100, 106, 126, 131 and 143.

What's in a Mindset?

A mindset is a set of beliefs, principles and values which influence the way you see the world. Adopting a particular mindset is like putting on a pair of glasses – a set of lenses which modify your vision, sharpening some things and blurring others.

We think the five characteristics we've just shared beat intelligence hands down. And they form a mindset that's going to put you in the best position for success. This is the student mindset.

The VESPA Circle

Where do you think you sit at the moment? It's worth spending time thinking about which VESPA elements you might be strong in and which elements you might need to strengthen.

This is a simple activity to get you thinking about VESPA and to help you figure out where you might need to develop. First, consider the statements below on the continuum. Think of the line as being a 1–10 scale.

Vision:

1	10
I don't like setting goals and targets.	I always set goals for myself.
I tend not to stick to goals I've set myself.	I always finish everything I start.

Effort:

1	10
I don't like working hard.	I'm extremely hard working.
I get easily distracted.	I'm very focused when I work.

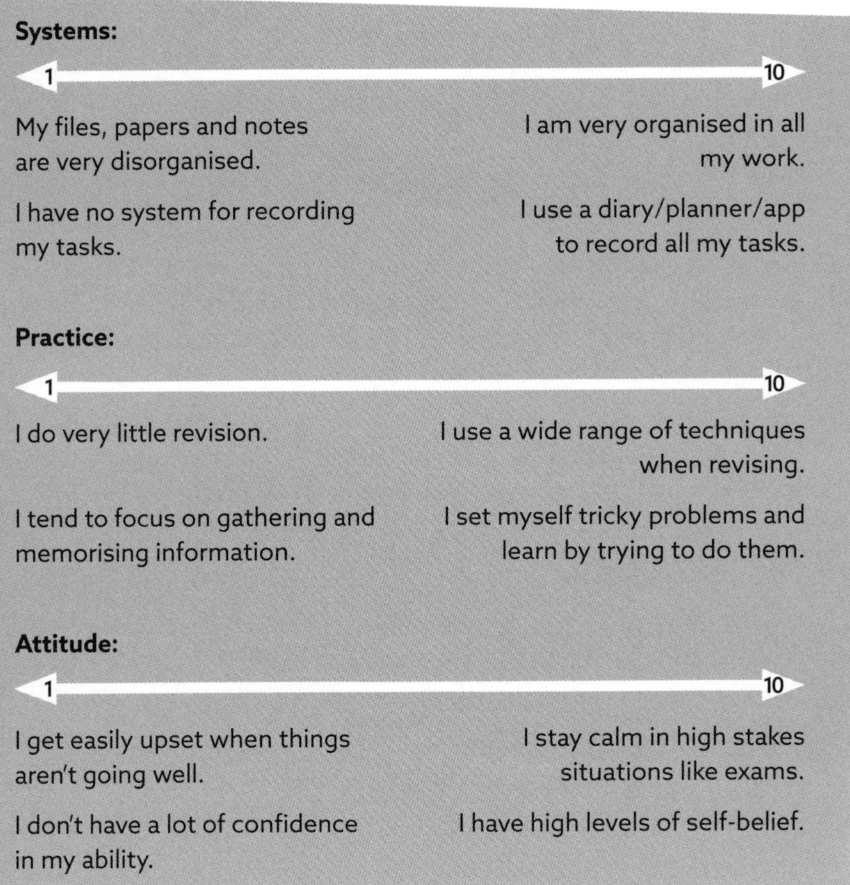

Systems:

1 ⟷ 10

My files, papers and notes are very disorganised. | I am very organised in all my work.

I have no system for recording my tasks. | I use a diary/planner/app to record all my tasks.

Practice:

1 ⟷ 10

I do very little revision. | I use a wide range of techniques when revising.

I tend to focus on gathering and memorising information. | I set myself tricky problems and learn by trying to do them.

Attitude:

1 ⟷ 10

I get easily upset when things aren't going well. | I stay calm in high stakes situations like exams.

I don't have a lot of confidence in my ability. | I have high levels of self-belief.

Now you've assessed the statements, try to assign a rough numerical value for each element of VESPA between 1 and 10. Then simply shade in the section on the profile opposite, working from the inside out.

Figure I.1. The VESPA circle

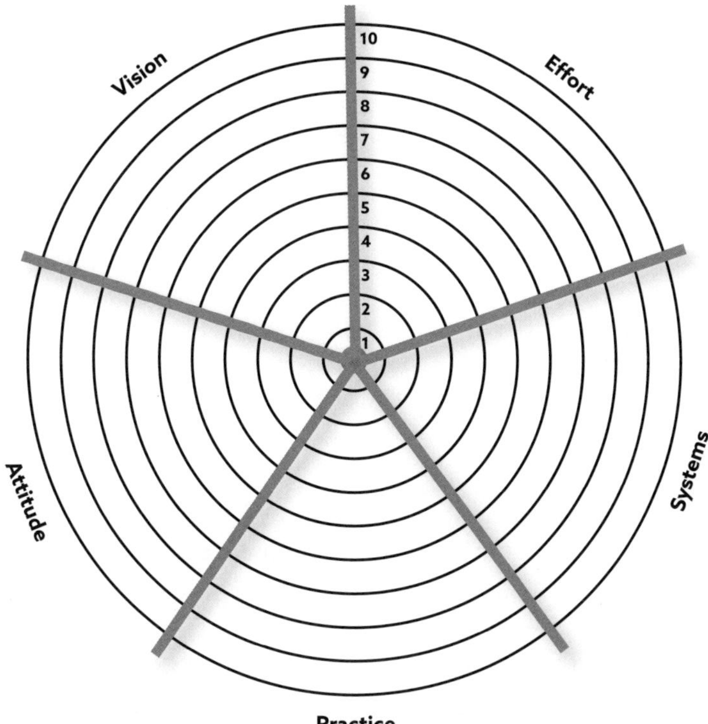

Now you've got a visual sense of where you are, you might want to pay particular attention to certain activities as you work through this book. When you come across one that deals with an area you might feel weaker in, give it your full focus.

Experiment as you go along. Some activities might look potentially uncomfortable, but give them your time anyway. Some might need a couple of attempts before you get to grips with them. Others might not suit you at all. That's fine. Select the ones that work for you, adjust them if necessary and you can create your own toolkit of strategies and tactics.

How This Book Works

There's an array of studies examining precisely how learning occurs, and we've found them really helpful in assessing where we're succeeding and where we might be going wrong in our own learning. A significant number of studies conclude that learning happens in steps. Many scholars have suggested that we pass through phases when we are learning something academic. Fitts and Posner (1967) studied motor skills in athletes and observed them mastering techniques in stages.*

Cooper, Sullivan and Shulman (1978), working at Michigan State University, looked at academic learning and also saw learners passing through distinct stages. Haring, Lovitt, Eaton and Hansen (1978) discovered the same.

We've researched and combined the results of these studies, plus a number of other models, to develop the six-section sequence that follows. It describes the phases you're likely to go through as you explore your new subject, course or topic. At each phase you'll experience challenges and discover new ways of working. You'll have particular questions, issues or worries.

We've organised the book using these six phases so you can recognise which phase you're in, and choose some tools to help you get through it.

1 **Preparation – getting ready to learn (Chapter 1)**

Preparation is often overlooked but it should occur before each extended period of learning.

Questions: What's my mindset like at the moment? Am I in a good frame of mind? What should I expect? What are my obstacles to success going to be? How might I need to learn?

* Cited in Wulf (2007), p. 3.

2 Starting study – beginning the learning process (Chapter 2)

This happens at least three times, since after every period of downtime you're required to get yourself revved up and refocused all over again.

Questions: What am I trying to achieve? Why? What does success look like for me? Has anyone else done it before? What might I learn from their experiences?

3 Collecting and shaping – gathering your information (Chapter 3)

Collecting and shaping starts from day one and doesn't end until the final months of your course, at which point you'll stop assimilating new information and work with what you've got.

Questions: What's my most important information? How can I arrange and organise it all? How are things connected? What are the key ideas and principles? How can I recast this material so it feels like mine?

4 Adapting, testing and performing – using your information to achieve outcomes (Chapter 4)

This begins later – you need a body of knowledge before you can practise effectively – but it goes on right until the final hour.

Questions: How do I create a robust working knowledge of everything I've learned? How do I demonstrate my mastery of this material and use it under pressure? How do I prepare and practise?

5 Flow and feedback – getting better through focused practice (Chapter 5)

This is the zone where you seek to practise intensely in order to improve your skills. This stage usually comes later in a course, but some learners reach it more quickly.

Questions: Is there a level above where I am? How do I access it? Can I get some perspective and see what's going well and what isn't? Why do others seem to be in the zone and I'm not? Are there better, quicker ways to do this?

Dealing with the dip – handling setbacks and solving study-related problems (Chapter 6)

The dip is the place where problems occur and motivation weakens. It happens at different times for different people, but we're always aware of its presence.

Questions: Everything feels like it's going wrong – how do I get out of this? Is it just me? Are there systems to help me get through these difficult times?

These phases don't come one after the other. They co-exist – like this:

Figure I.2. The six phases of learning

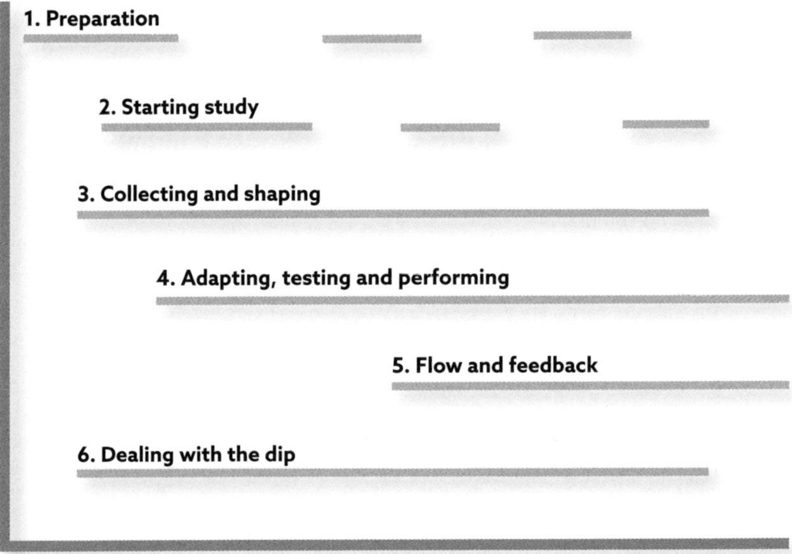

So, for lots of the time you'll be doing all six at once.

CHAPTER 1
Preparation

Questions:
What's my mindset like at the moment?
Am I in a good frame of mind?
What should I expect?
What are my obstacles to success going to be?
How might I need to learn?

Key elements of the VESPA model in this phase:
vision and attitude.

Dr Tina Seelig, author of the excellent book *inGenius: A Crash Course on Creativity*, teaches a course on creativity at Harvard. Her course is very popular - every year she has to turn some applicants down.

One year, Seelig received a note from a student who hadn't made it onto the course. 'He said that he *never* gets into the courses he wants,' Seelig writes. 'I thought carefully about how to respond and sent him the following message: "If there is a course you really want to take and you don't get a spot in the class, then just keep showing up. Spots usually open up during the first week ... If you're there, you're almost guaranteed the spot."'

'Thank you for this advice,' the student wrote back. 'I assume that won't work for your class.' Seelig continues, 'I stared at his email for several minutes and then responded, "Yes, you're right. It won't work." I had handed him the ruby slippers and he didn't take them.'

Seelig contrasts this with a second student whose application was also unsuccessful, but who wrote to ask if she could attend just one class. When a student later dropped out, she got the place.

'The difference between them,' Seelig concludes, 'is their attitude. The first fellow ... didn't even see the possibility when I placed it in front of him. The second student created a way to get what she wanted' (Seelig, 2012, pp. 169–170).

The right attitude created an opening for the student who was able to see it. The direction of her life changed because she took advantage of the opportunities available to her.

Getting your preparation right helps you to see opportunities. Consider the first example on page 17:

Attitude	Emotional response to challenge	Decisions and behaviour	Results
I don't feel in control of my destiny. Other people seem to get chances and opportunities I don't.	I've developed 'selective attention' about chances to try new and interesting things. I didn't even see the posters advertising that particular competition. Now it's pretty much the deadline for entries.	I get the information but I know it's already too late. I don't bother entering. A fellow student on my course does enter, and wins. The first prize is £1,000.	I miss out, and I reinforce my belief that good things only happen to other people.

Or this one:

Attitude	Emotional response to challenge	Decisions and behaviour	Results
I'm highly likely to see criticism of my work as criticism of myself.	I've had a low mark and a list of things to improve, but I feel angry and indignant.	I'm going to tell myself I don't care. My tutors are wrong and this course is unfair. I'm not going to put much effort into improving the work because it feels uncomfortable and embarrassing.	I get a lower grade than others, and can't access a particular course module/ get into a particular class/get a particular job as a result.

As these examples demonstrate, preparation is a crucial part of the journey. By knowing yourself – who you are and what you're trying to achieve – you can anticipate and avoid a number of the obstacles ahead.

Before you take your first step, here are three key activities to have a go at. It can be tempting to skip this part and travel straight to the next phase, but even half an hour or so spent here can make a difference.

1. Vision Activity: The Learner's Manifesto

A manifesto is a statement of intent, like a resolution. If you make yourself a personal manifesto and commit it to paper, it's like the start of building yourself a new mindset. It becomes like your operating system. The apps at the surface of your life may change, but underneath your manifesto and mindset contain the principles that make your operating system run glitch-free every day.

Before building your manifesto, consider the following:

* The 'beginner's mind' is a phrase meaning a quality of approach to study that we can all have – seeking to be open, eager and uncritical. 'In the beginner's mind,' says Shunryu Suzuki, 'there are many possibilities, but in the expert's there are few' (Suzuki, 2005, p. 1).
* Naturalist Rachel Carson expresses it this way: 'A child's world is fresh and new and beautiful, full of wonder and excitement. It is our misfortune ... [that] that true instinct ... is dimmed and even lost before we reach adulthood' (Carson, 1965, p. 42).
* Or if you want your advice research-based, try Professor Victor Ottati's paper – in the *Journal of Experimental Social Psychology*, no less. The more expert someone feels, he says, the more closed-minded they are likely to be. In the prof's words, 'situations that [create] self-perceptions of high expertise elicit a more closed-minded cognitive style' (Ottati et al., 2015, p. 1).

The good news is that we can all return to the position of beginner, even if we're starting something as advanced as a degree in a particular subject.

Here are the five inherent dispositions of the beginner's mind:

1. **Discard fear of failure;** instead expect it.
2. **Be comfortable with 'I don't know'.** Your mind is ready for new thoughts, not rehashing old ones. Get comfortable with 'that doesn't make sense'. Turn it into 'that doesn't make sense *yet*'. See if you can hold opposing, illogical ideas in your head for long periods. It's safe to assume that you're going to study something that might not make sense for a week, a month or even longer. Disregard 'common sense' preconceptions or 'what I thought was true'. Most people's early education has dealt in *strategically simplified versions of the truth*.
3. **Seek out divergent thinking.** There are many possibilities and many answers, not just one. Others may have persuasive opinions; you don't need to wholeheartedly agree with them.
4. **Be curious and enquiring.** Replace 'I'm dreading this!' with 'I wonder what this will be like?' Focus on questions rather than answers.
5. Psychologist Abraham Maslow said we should **try to think 'without fashions, fads, dogmas, habits or other pictures-in-the-head of what is proper, normal, "right"'.** Instead, we should be 'ready to receive whatever happens to be the case without surprise, shock, indignation or denial' (Maslow, 2000, p. 194).

Your learner's manifesto should describe the best version of you – how that best version learns, what attitudes you bring to learning and how they work. The ideal operating system.

There are plenty of examples out there. Here are a few to give you a sense of what you're looking for:

* Farnam Street – an organisation devoted to helping users 'develop an understanding of how the world really works, make better decisions, and live a better life' – has five principles: 'direction over speed', 'live deliberately', 'thoughtful opinions held loosely', 'principles outlive tactics' and 'own your own actions'.*

---

* See https://fs.blog/principles/.

- The manifesto of the Indie Travel group (who believe that 'we better understand ourselves and others when we leave home to experience the world first-hand') is created by forum discussion followed by up or down voting statements. Under discussion at the time of writing are: 'pack light and keep things simple', 'replace broad expectations with nuanced realities', 'options over possessions' and 'discovery over escape'.*
- Leo Tolstoy, the author of *War and Peace*, wrote his own manifesto when he was 18. Here are some of our favourite bits: 'Get up early (5 o'clock)'; 'Eat little and avoid sweets'; 'Try to do everything by yourself'; 'Have a goal for your whole life, a goal for one section of your life, a goal for a shorter period and a goal for the year; a goal for every month, a goal for every week, a goal for every day'; 'Be good, but try to let no one know it'; and 'Always live less expensively than you might'.†

If that isn't inspiration enough, here are some other areas you might want to consider when formulating your manifesto:

- Effort and efficiency: 'I give 100%, whatever I do. I never give up. I don't waste time. I get things done.'
- Resilience: 'I'm dedicated. I'm strong under pressure. People can rely on me.'
- Wealth of resources: 'I'm going to ask for help and advice every day. I'm going to get the most out of all the resources around me.'
- Agency: 'It's down to me to fix problems and chase down solutions. I don't pass on responsibility when things get tough.'
- The beginner's mind: 'I'm positive, open-minded and curious. I welcome mistakes and feedback.'

---

* See http://indietravel.org/.

† See https://gretchenrubin.com/2011/01/10-rules-of-life-from-tolstoy-what-are-your-rules/. Tolstoy's 'Rules of Life' appear in Henri Troyat's biography, *Tolstoy* (2001 [1967]).

Design your manifesto here:

Once you've chosen your new operating system, you need to find a method of verbalising it, of remembering it and retelling it to yourself. The term 'mantra' is often used to describe an utterance or phrase with psychological power. This is what you're creating here – a shortened version of your manifesto.

Summarise it in one sentence or phrase:

. . . .

. . . .

. . . .

. . . .

Find a time of day when you can repeat your mantra – in the shower, on the bus, walking home or crossing the campus between lectures.

2. Attitude Activity: The Five Glitches

Even with the best of intentions, we might find ourselves suddenly assailed by doubt or fear when beginning our studies. One of the ways to best tackle these anxieties is to try to classify them, so we can easily recognise them when they emerge.

In this activity, we refer to these doubts and fears as 'glitches'. We've chosen this metaphor of a software bug because we've found it helpful in rethinking what's happening when we feel overwhelmed.

Have a look at the following glitches which are common among students:

1 **The glitch of belonging**
This glitch works by promoting how important it is to be normal. It tells you that your value comes from your ability to conform and belong. If you're normal, you'll be welcomed and accepted. Then the glitch not-so-helpfully highlights all the ways in which you're *not* normal: everyone's got higher grades than you. They're using words you don't understand. You just don't belong. This glitch is masterful at conjuring up what psychologists call 'imposter syndrome' – the feeling that you've faked your way into a job or course.

2 **The twin glitches of comfort and ease**
These glitches start by promoting the joys of cosiness, and then draw your attention to potential discomfort. They're the ones making you look at the rain outside, or reminding you how cold it will be if your train is late, or how comfortable your bed is. Their aim is to create inertia.

3 **The glitch of helplessness**
This glitch works by convincing you that the locus of control for your life lies outside you. It tells you that you're not the architect of your own destiny, and it's down to others to ensure you're on

track. When you're in a jam, this glitch lines up a list of people to blame: the library didn't have that crucial textbook just when you needed it, or the lecturer moved that lecture and never told you about it, or someone stole your reading list.

4 **The glitch of perfection**
This glitch begins by drawing your attention to the importance of polished perfection. Assignments need to be graded as close to 100% as possible. This glitch often refers to your past. It tells you that you've never made any significant mistakes up to this point, so you should continue to be perfect. You wouldn't want to put that record at risk, would you?

5 **The glitch of status**
This glitch works by promoting the notion that status is everything. Status is conferred by others and so the opinion of peers is crucially important. The glitch waits until you're in a situation where you have to choose between maintaining your status or being successful. It then tries its best to make sure you choose status over success, so you keep the good opinion of your peers but fail your course.

Which glitches have you faced before? What happened? Who won?

. . . .

. . . .

. . . .

. . . .

. . . .

. . . .

. . . .

. . . .

Which glitches are likely to return? Put the five in order, from most likely to least likely to be an obstacle:

....

....

....

....

....

Do the five glitches listed here cover everything, or are there other glitches? Record them in the table on page 26.

Now that you've considered your potential obstacles, you might need to rewrite your operating system - your learner's manifesto - to strengthen it against further attack.

Return to Activity 1 and reconsider what you've said so far.

Glitch	It tricks me into thinking ...	The result might be that I ...

3. Attitude Activity: The ABC of Fear

All of us feel fear at some point in our lives. Fear about a goal often stops us taking any action.

The American psychologist Albert Ellis (1957) had a really interesting way of dealing with fear. He argued that fear is a response to an *activating event* (A) – something happens which makes us fearful. It might be a test or an exam. It might be a challenging seminar with high level thinking and discussion. It might be a lecture about applications for postgraduate study. Whatever it is, it triggers anxiety.

Then, Ellis argued, the anxiety triggers a *belief* (B). This may be a false belief that has been learned over the years, but it can be deep-seated and persistent. A and B collide to give C, a *consequence*. We subconsciously choose a certain behaviour and act it out. This is Ellis' ABC model of irrational beliefs.

An example might look like this:

A **Activating event**: There's a lecture about the challenges of the undergraduate year and how hard you'll need to work to be successful.

B **Belief**: Over the years you've acquired a false belief that you can't motivate yourself to work hard.

C **Consequence**: You immediately feel that study at this level will be impossible for you. You decide you don't care, you don't want to be successful, you're not enjoying your course anyway. You work less hard than others.

How might we break this cycle? Ellis offers two other letters, D and E, to give us some guidance here. D stands for *dispute*. What can we do to dispute the belief we have about ourselves? Do we have any evidence to show us that our false belief is wrong? He then recommends that we get an *energising alternative* (E) to the false belief - a new, more positive belief about ourselves.

Take some time to think about yourself, and use the space below to make some notes.

A Have there been any activating events that have made you feel anxious in the past? List them. Do they have anything in common? Do they make you feel anxious because they trigger a long-held false belief about yourself?

....

....

....

....

....

B What false beliefs might you have developed about yourself over the years? Why have these beliefs begun to feel real?

....

....

....

....

....

C Make a list of actions you've taken at some point in your past as a consequence of a false belief. Have these actions made the false belief seem even more real?

....

. . . .

. . . .

. . . .

. . . .

D Imagine you had to completely destroy your false belief. What arguments would you make? What evidence could you use?

. . . .

. . . .

. . . .

. . . .

. . . .

E What energising alternatives to your false belief could you generate?

. . . .

. . . .

. . . .

. . . .

. . . .

You might want to return to your manifesto (Activity 1) at this point and rework it in light of the thinking you've done.

CHAPTER 2

Starting Study

Questions:
What's this all for?
What am I trying to achieve?
Why?
What does success look like?
Has anyone else done it before?

Key elements of the VESPA model in this phase:
vision and attitude.

Undertaking any study usually takes time. Some courses can be completed within a few weeks; a PhD, by contrast, might take you five to ten years. Before you start, it's worth thinking about *why* you're actually starting. We've worked with hundreds of students who haven't really thought through their why, and quite often they are the first to find that they've signed up for the wrong course or when the going gets tough they simply give up. Those with a real appetite for what they want to do are the ones who usually succeed.

In order to explore this more closely, let's imagine two university students beginning the same course. The first student isn't sure of their why; they just have a what: 'I'm studying medicine at university. I want to be a doctor.'

The second one has a clear why. They commit to a problem and purpose, expressed as a series of questions: 'Is public healthcare in the UK consistently excellent? If not, why not? How can I improve the situation for patients from all walks of life?'

There are weaknesses, like fault lines, embedded in the first student's goal. One bad year sees the entire plan destroyed. Often the student knows this; they're jumpy, anxious and stressed. Everything depends on this one result. The joy they might have felt for their subject has gone. The energetic research, reading and thinking that might have once occurred is sacrificed for just getting the result.

The second student, meanwhile, knows there are uncontrollables ahead - exam questions they can't predict, interview curveballs that are impossible to anticipate. It doesn't matter; they know their purpose and the problems that interest them in the world. That's the direction of travel, and if there are obstacles along the way, they'll work out how to overcome them or adjust course to pass them by.

So, what's your why?

We asked a number of students to spend some time thinking not about their what (a course or a specific job) but their why - a problem they saw in the world and wanted to solve. Looking at other people's whys might help you to decide on your own why. This is what they came up with:

* How do we make the distribution of wealth in the UK fairer?
* How can we save larger numbers of species from extinction?
* How might we design buildings that increase people's happiness and well-being?
* What are the elements necessary for a critically acclaimed movie?
* How can we improve pupils' experience of school?
* How can the design of _____ be improved?
* How can we accelerate our progress towards curing _____?
* How can art be used to improve people's lives?
* How can I create popular, immersive and interactive computer games?
* How can we reduce crime by working with young offenders?
* What qualities make some _____ better than others?
* How can we help people to cope with difficult, stressful or traumatic times in their lives?
* What does outstanding parenting/teaching look like?
* How can we discover more about the workings of the universe?
* How do we solve global warming?
* What does augmented/virtual reality mean for media/entertainment/gaming?
* How can we work more efficiently using morally programmed artificial intelligence?

Once you think you have a few interesting problems that you'd like to explore further, you'll need to sketch out some next steps. Is there a documentary you could watch? A book you could read? Someone you could talk to or ask for advice? A piece of research you can do to get more information?

In this chapter, we'll try to put your why to the test. The activities that follow are going to really make you think about why you're going to commit time, effort and probably money to your chosen course. We're going to start by looking at what motivates you and check that you're on the right path and have the appetite to study. The word 'path' here is no coincidence – a number of these activities use the metaphor of a journey, road or route to help you decide on a way forward.

These activities aren't always fun; they might make you feel uncomfortable. Just keep going. By the end of the chapter you'll know if you have the appetite or not.

4. Vision Activity: The Motivation Diamond

What's the why behind everything you do? This might seem like quite a philosophical question, but sometimes it's easier to express the motivations and desires that are important to us rather than the jobs or courses that might fulfil them. Professor Steven Reiss (2000), who worked as a psychologist at Ohio State University, conducted studies with over 6,000 people to try to define their underlying motivations. He concluded his work by suggesting there are sixteen different motivations that guide all human behaviour. We've adjusted his list a little to make it more accessible and easy to work with. There are fifteen in ours.

Study the list below and decide which seem as though they might be the most important to you. Once you've shortlisted nine of the fifteen, you then have to prioritise them using the diamond on page 37. At the top of the diamond, leading the others, should be the motivation that beats all others for you. Underneath, you can have two deputies alongside each other. Then come the rest.

Here are the fifteen possible motivations (adapted from Steven Reiss for the purposes of this task):

1. **Acceptance:** the need for approval, support and good feeling from those around you.
2. **Competition:** the need to pit yourself against others – to compete and win.
3. **Curiosity:** the need to learn, explore, research, discover and try new things.
4. **Creativity:** the need to design, write, draw and build – to create art or entertainment.

5 **Family:** the need to raise or help children, to nurture others or to work in small, loyal units supporting those around you.

6 **Honour:** the need to be loyal to the key values of a group or society – to observe the rules, do what is expected and guide others in these values.

7 **Idealism:** the need for fairness, equality and social justice.

8 **Independence:** the need for individuality – the ability to organise and run things your way.

9 **Order:** the need for organised, stable, predictable environments; creating routines and patterns.

10 **Physical activity:** the need for movement, exercise and physical challenge.

11 **Power:** the need for influence, the ability to determine the direction of others and the responsibility for the performance of groups.

12 **Saving:** the need to collect things, to own things and to categorise or order them.

13 **Social contact:** the need for friends and to have extensive peer relationships.

14 **Social status:** the need to appear to be of a high social standing or a person of importance.

15 **Tranquillity:** the need to be calm, relaxed and safe.

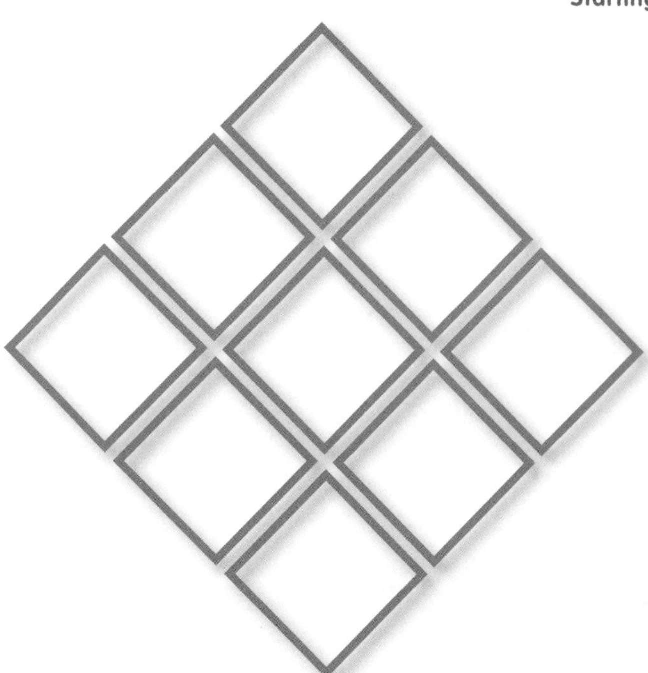

Once you've drawn up your leading motivations, think about how these link to the course that you're about to start.

What are your top three motivations? Do they link in any way? If so, how?

. . . .

. . . .

. . . .

If they don't link to your course, does this make you think differently about what you are about to embark on?

. . . .

. . . .

. . . .

5. Vision Activity: The Five Roads

This is another activity to help you check your why. All you need to do is imagine yourself at a junction with five possible ways forward: each way forward represents a possible choice for you. The aim of this activity is to make those possible choices clearer. This will enable you to objectively review your options, which is the first step in making a good decision. Don't feel a decision has to be made yet – it doesn't. But knowing what options are in play is always helpful.

Use the diagram below to think about what might lie at the end of each road. You might need to spend some time thinking about these, and you could begin by scribbling two or three options at the tip of each road before coming to add more or cross others off as your preferences become clearer.

Having done this, note down your thoughts in more detail in the spaces provided on pages 39–41.

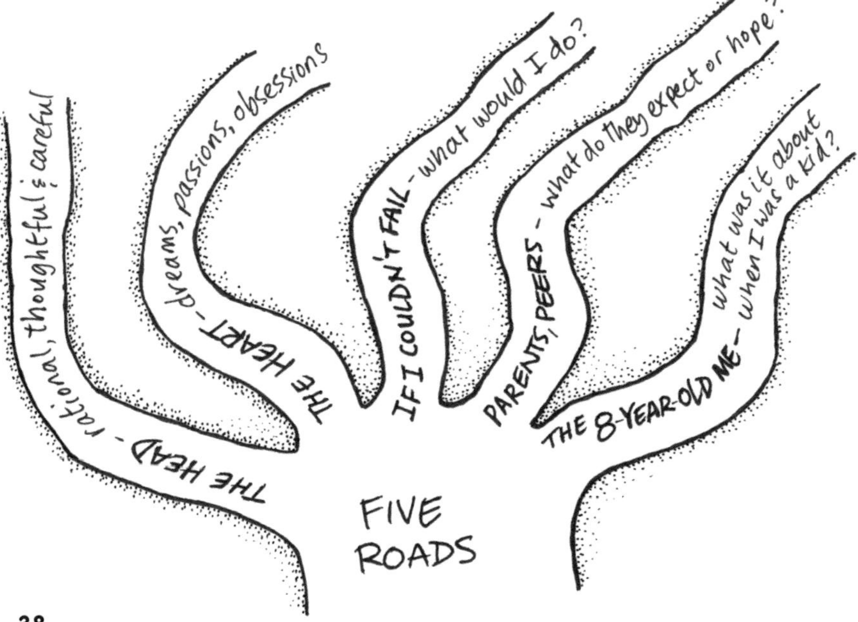

1 **The head.** Here, note down the choices that occur to you when you think rationally. This is the careful and thoughtful road. There will be low risk on this road – it's safe and certain – so it might not be your most exciting road forward.

....

....

....

....

....

....

2 **The heart.** This road is about wholeheartedly pursuing your passions; the studying that makes you excited and that you would willingly spend time on for free. This might be a riskier road, with greater levels of uncertainty, but you'll be fired up as well as slightly fearful as you travel it.

....

....

....

....

....

....

3 **If I couldn't fail.** At the end of this imaginary road is guaranteed success in something. It will be a hard road to travel, and there may be tough times, but it will end in 100% success. In other words, if you knew you couldn't fail at something, what would you choose to do?

....

....

....

....

....

....

4 **Parents, peers.** Here, consider what others are expecting of you. You may be surrounded by people with strong opinions – lecturers, tutors, parents and extended family – all telling you that you have to pursue a certain course or that you're a natural at something. You might, or might not, agree with them. Make a note of all the things you feel a pressure to pursue.

....

....

....

....

....

....

5 **The 8-year-old me.** If you'd done this activity at primary school, what would you have said you wanted to do in the future? Often, we find that elements of our early passions persist; you might write something down here and suddenly remember a passion that you've forgotten or forced yourself to ignore. Maybe it's time to revisit it, or maybe there are just parts of it that are still relevant today.

Once you've got some ideas scribbled down at the end of each road, let these thoughts develop for a few days.

Finally, don't feel you need to make a decision yet. Just knowing the possible ways forward puts you in a strong position. And when you travel a road, it doesn't mean you can never return to try another. You can!

How does this activity affect or change your thinking?

6. Vision Activity: The Interview

Some courses require an interview of some description, so you might have already gone through this process. If you haven't had an interview, it's worth doing this activity to check you have the right appetite for studying. Whenever we've interviewed students, the ones with genuine enthusiasm stand out a mile. They've usually thought through questions similar to the ones below and find it quite easy to answer them.

In this activity, imagine you're being interviewed at the end of the first month on your programme of study. Just block out some time, find a quiet space and write the answers in the spaces provided. You might even ask a friend to interview you and get them to rate your answers.

Here goes:

1 Which part of your education have you enjoyed the most? What were you studying? *Top tip: Try to link aspects of your previous study to the present course – are there any similarities?*

. . . .

. . . .

. . . .

2 How would you have felt if you'd missed out on the course you're now on?

. . . .

. . . .

. . . .

3 What has been your motivation to complete this course of study?

. . . .

. . . .

. . . .

4 What aspect of the course do you find exciting?

. . . .

. . . .

. . . .

5 How will you be assessed on the course? Is this your preferred method?

. . . .

. . . .

. . . .

6 If you were in charge of assessment on this course, what would it look like?

. . . .

. . . .

. . . .

7 Do you know anyone who has already been on the course? How did they find it?

. . . .

. . . .

. . . .

8 If you were in charge of creating the ultimate course, what would the programme of study look like?

. . . .

. . . .

. . . .

9 What was the last book you read on the subject area?

. . . .

. . . .

. . . .

10 Why do you want to do the course?

. . . .

. . . .

. . . .

Now that you've completed the first three activities in this chapter you should be clear on your why. Can you see any themes developing? It's worth scanning over your answers to look for patterns. A good way to do this is to record the information in the table below. Use the interests and passions column to record your positive responses - things that are positively linked to your course - and the dislikes column to record any negative responses - things that don't seem to fit with your chosen path.

Interests and passions	Dislikes

Now it's time for some deep reflection:

* Does everything in your interests and passions column match your course?
* Has anything that's surfaced in the dislikes column made you rethink your choice?

7. Vision Activity: The Roadmap

Now that you are clear on your why, it's time to take action and set some goals related to your learning. What do you want to achieve, and how are you going to achieve it?

Sometimes setting a goal can feel like a long process. The goals can seem so distant that we don't take any immediate action. Designing a success map can really help with this. A success map is a visual reminder of the journey you're going on. It guides you to where you want to be and warns you about things that might pull you off course.

Here's what you need to do. First, you need to go to the end of the map and write down the goal you want to achieve. This might be applying for a specific course or it might be the grade you want to get at the end of it. In the same box it's useful to include the date by which you want to attain your goal. Underneath the goal box you'll see 'Why'. Here you write why achieving the goal is important to you. This should be easy if you've done the first three activities.

Next, you need to break down these stages into a series of steps in a journey over a period of days, weeks or even months. Represent them as a road or pathway – some sort of track that takes you through the difficulties and towards a conclusion.

Once done, it's a good idea to keep your map on display somewhere you can always see it. This will help to remind you of the steps that need to be completed to reach that destination in the distance!

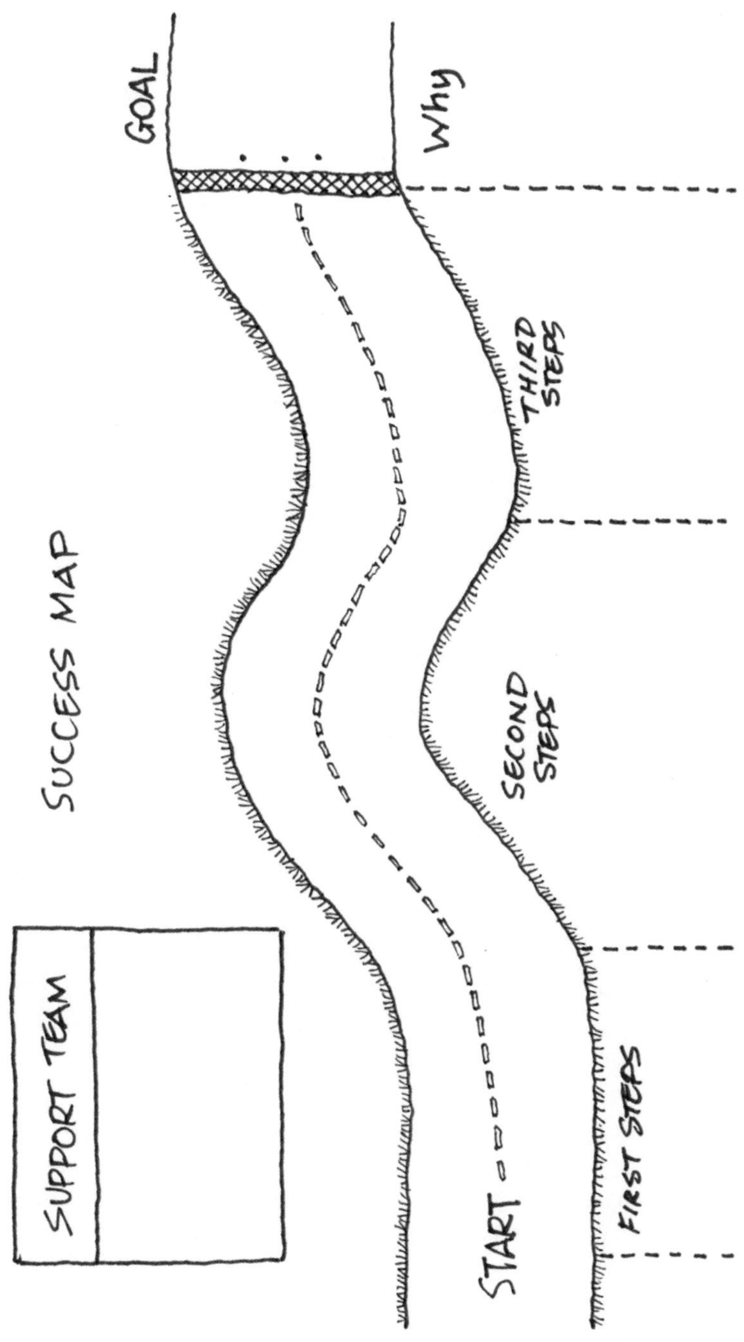
SUCCESS MAP
SUPPORT TEAM
GOAL
Why
THIRD STEPS
SECOND STEPS
FIRST STEPS
START

8. Vision Activity: Weekly Rule of Three

We borrowed this activity from Jack Canfield's book *The Success Principles* (2005). Canfield employs the useful analogy of chopping down a tree when trying to achieve your goals. He says that if you take a very sharp axe and take three swings at a tree every day, no matter how big the tree, eventually it will come down. It's the same with any goal you set. If you take a few small steps every month towards achieving your goal, eventually you'll get there, no matter how big the goal.

Canfield almost makes it sound inevitable. It makes you think: the reason people don't achieve their dreams isn't that they lack a dream, it's that they just don't take any action. *A dream is just a dream unless you take action.*

This activity might seem simple, but we can vouch for it as being one of the most effective tools we have ever used.

All you have to do is take three steps every week towards achieving your long-term goal. It's that simple. You just have to decide the steps you are going to take and then commit to doing them.

First, remind yourself of your long-term goal:

My goal is:

....

Then list all the actions that are going to take you closer to achieving that goal. Remember, it's only three small steps per week. It doesn't matter how small, as long as you are taking action. You can record these at the start of your diary each week or use the following table for the first three weeks.

Week 1	
	....
	....
	....
	....
	....
	....
Week 2	
	....
	....
	....
	....
	....
	....
Week 3	
	....
	....
	....
	....
	....
	....

When you've completed the table, it's important to keep it somewhere you can see it. Stick it up in your room or study area.

9. Attitude Activity: The Rocky Road

You're now clear on your why, but you still might have some doubts and fears about the journey ahead. Two psychologists from the University of Miami, Robert Emmons and Michael McCullough (2003), asked this question: what if we reviewed stressful and difficult times and turned our attention to the lessons we learned from those negative experiences?

Three hundred students were asked to recollect challenging periods of their lives: poor results, breaking up with a partner, feeling insulted or offended, being rejected from a particular course. Of the 300 subjects, 100 were asked to specifically focus on the lessons they had learned – the positive benefits that had eventually come from their ordeals. It turned out that it was these students who coped better with their disasters and moved on from them. Emmons and McCullough found that positive benefits could flow from negative experiences.

David Collins, professor of coaching and performance at the University of Central Lancashire, has coached at the very top level, including being responsible for UK athletics at the Beijing Olympic Games. Collins, with his colleague Áine MacNamara, has done similar work to Emmons and McCullough (Collins and MacNamara, 2012). He's discovered that top athletes have travelled what he calls a 'rocky road'. This means they've usually had their fair share of setbacks, failures and disappointments along the way. Often, we don't get to hear about these setbacks – we only hear about the successes.

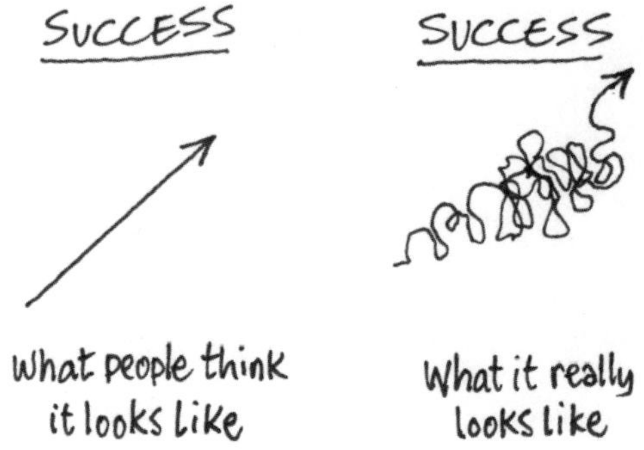

Professor Collins suggests that the rocky road might even be good for you as you will develop some useful skills along the way. The key point is not to dwell on the setback and to bounce back.

Your study period is going to bring challenges and difficulties, but you can use them as fuel. Think about a recent negative experience (e.g. a disappointing exam result, a period when you became demotivated or lacked direction) and consider the eight points below. For each, spend some time reflecting. Don't expect all eight to work for you - perhaps three or four will help you to see the experience more positively. Making notes might help to clarify your thinking too. Think about:

1. A personal quality you didn't have that you've now begun to develop.
2. An increased appreciation of some part of your life as a result of what has happened.
3. A realisation you might never have considered before the experience.
4. An increased confidence about the way the world, or certain people, work.
5. A skill you've developed or that has been enhanced as a result of the experience - such as thinking through problems, reflecting and understanding, communicating ideas or arguing confidently.
6. A relationship that has been strengthened (perhaps with someone who helped or supported you through the experience) or improved (for instance, with someone who hurt you).
7. A 'rule' or lesson you have extracted from the experience that you can now apply in new situations.
8. A reassessment of certain priorities.

This task should remind you that we grow as a result of difficult times. Keep it somewhere close and refer to it when you need to.

CHAPTER 3

Collecting and Shaping

Questions:
In all of this stuff I've got, what's important?
How can I arrange and organise it all?
How are things connected?
What are the key ideas and principles?
How does it all work together?

Key elements of the VESPA model in this phase:
effort and systems.

Collecting and organising new information can be overwhelming. It takes effort – there's no shortcut to processing and consuming new material. You'll need to set aside the hours to get it done. The good news is that three or four sessions in and already you will be feeling better. The fear of the work is way worse than the work itself.

It calls for systems. You'll have to work with a set of tools to make sense of what you're seeing. You'll be recording it (or there's no point), so you'll be using notes, diagrams, tables, charts and other graphic organisers. Then you'll be connecting it, recasting it and making sense of it, so it works for you. The strategies in this chapter focus on these two elements, giving you a toolkit of approaches with which to experiment.

Here's a helpful way to think about learning: new information is like new territory, so learning is akin to exploring a new city or unlocking a new level on a computer game. Tim Urban, creator of long-form info website waitbutwhy.com, knows all about learning. His job is to read lots of disparate material, learn it and then re-present it as a long-form essay – a simple explanation of something usually considered dauntingly complex.

Urban has an interesting metaphor about new territory – he compares the process to entering a room in the dark. You stumble in, blind. You can't see a thing. You feel overwhelmed and fearful. Urban says, 'I always start feeling like I'm blindfolded in a room and I'm just trying to figure out where are even the walls here.'* In other words, where are the edges of this topic? When is something *not* this topic?

Urban uses Wikipedia ('It's good at telling you where the walls are'). The articles give you the key information you need, and each one has a bunch of links at the bottom. Read and take notes for a few hours (both articles and selected links), and the walls of the room

* All the quotes are from Tim Ferriss' interview with Tim Urban (Ferriss, 2017a).

are becoming pretty clear – the lights have come on and the room is partially illuminated. What can you see?

Urban asks, 'Where is the furniture? I just want to understand what I even need to learn.' The tables and chairs are your core ideas – the ideas that seem important because they keep getting mentioned in articles and links. You'll need to know these well, following them up with separate searches. You will find plenty of other pieces of information at this point – ideas that don't seem to fit or make sense yet. This is all part of the process so don't worry – file them under 'unsolved' and carry on.

What about the foundations of the room or building? Urban has a neat way of exploring this. He suggests imagining the room – even when it's lit – as being constructed on sand, so it must be secured by deep vertical struts to stop it shifting. 'You need to build a foundation,' Urban says. Keep exploring what seems to be the most important information. Keep asking why – going deeper and deeper. Follow the references at the bottom of the Wikipedia pages, concentrating your searches on the key ideas and terms, as if you're driving a metal strut deep into the ground, so your room of information becomes strong and steady.

Then you fill in-between the struts where it looks interesting. You'll come across loads of contradictory information as you do this. There will be competing ideas, conflicting schools of thought, different beliefs. Don't worry – just make a note of them all so you can summarise them. As you go along, you'll begin to figure out who you trust.

Finally, Urban heads to YouTube – to take a break from reading by watching a talk, a lecture or an explanatory video. This is to 'round out' your understanding, to neaten it up and knock the edges off it. Your aim, he says, is to watch an entire YouTube video on the subject that doesn't teach you anything new. Once you've done that a few times, you know that your understanding is pretty solid.

10. Systems Activity: Mapping New Territory

Key terms or definitions:	Other terms – strange or currently confusing ideas:
Important thinkers:	A central text (e.g. academic paper, book, artwork) that gets mentioned regularly:
Crucial arguments or controversies – where is there disagreement?	Something/someone that keeps getting mentioned in research papers and articles:

Getting to grips with a new topic can be daunting. In the early stages, it's like being an explorer in a new landscape.

What are the key landmarks in your new territory? What seems to be emerging as important? The following table gives you the chance to gather your first impressions:

Important events:	Key dates/time periods, and why:
Two other texts that seem almost as important:	More minor texts/references:
Something your trusted sources indicate is important:	Core principles or ways of thinking:

There are only twelve boxes, so anything that sits outside the grid goes in your 'currently unsolved' list:

- ....
- ....
- ....
- ....
- ....
- ....
- ....
- ....
- ....
- ....
- ....
- ....
- ....
- ....
- ....
- ....
- ....
- ....

11. Systems Activity: Fifteen Graphic Organisers

How do we build connections between facts and ideas - and really get to grips with the information we have?

One way is by reorganising pieces of information. Graphic organisers can help you do this. For example, if you need to compare two topics/ideas, a simple two-column table headed with 'Similarities' and 'Differences' might be all you need. But if you wanted to summarise a series of opposing arguments or viewpoints, you would need to consider a more complex visual metaphor, perhaps from the list of suggestions on pages 60–62.

Five Simple Organisers

1. Make a mind-map of the information.
2. Make a comparison table and pull out similarities and differences between two studies, methods, people, characters or historical events.
3. Make a flow chart to summarise a process.
4. Make a graph to represent data.
5. Make a timeline showing a series of events including cause and effect.

Notice the focus on action here - each of our suggestions begins with 'make'. That's you being active, engaging with the information and reorganising it so that it becomes knowledge.

Five Complex Organisers

Alternatively, you can use complex graphic organisers. They usually take the form of a metaphor where you turn something into something else.

For example, summarise everything you know about a topic using the metaphor of a tree:

* What key information forms the trunk?
* What underlying information makes the roots?
* What are the important branches?
* What subsections of information become the twigs and leaves?

If this metaphor works for you, try the following five:

1. A castle with separate turrets and a strong foundation.
2. A stream growing into a river and then a lake. (There's an example of this coming up.)
3. A village with a central square and streets around it.
4. A clock face.
5. A mobile phone with apps.

Five Further Thoughts

The metaphors above are all physical objects. But some of the best metaphors to use are *processes*, with moving parts and things happening one after the other. Try summarising your learning using a process metaphor. We love these suggestions, which have been borrowed and adapted from Roger von Oech's book on creativity, *A Whack on the Side of the Head* (1992, p. 46):

1. **Cooking something.** What are the basic ingredients? How might they be combined? What is the cooking process? How will it be served at the end?
2. **Creating a colony on an empty island.** Who are the pioneers? What needs to be built first? How does agriculture work? What is the township like?
3. **Sailing through a storm.** What is the boat like? What are its sails made of? What ballast does it need to stay upright? What is the storm? How does the boat respond?
4. **Planting a garden.** What does the soil need to be like? What needs to be planted first? How will it grow and develop? What will be needed to sustain growth? What are the threats to further growth?

5 **Conducting an orchestra.** What are the components of the orchestra? How many musicians are there and how do they relate to each other? Who or what is the conductor? What makes great music? What's it like when it goes wrong?

The Student Mindset's guide to zombie fiction, as a stream, river and lake!

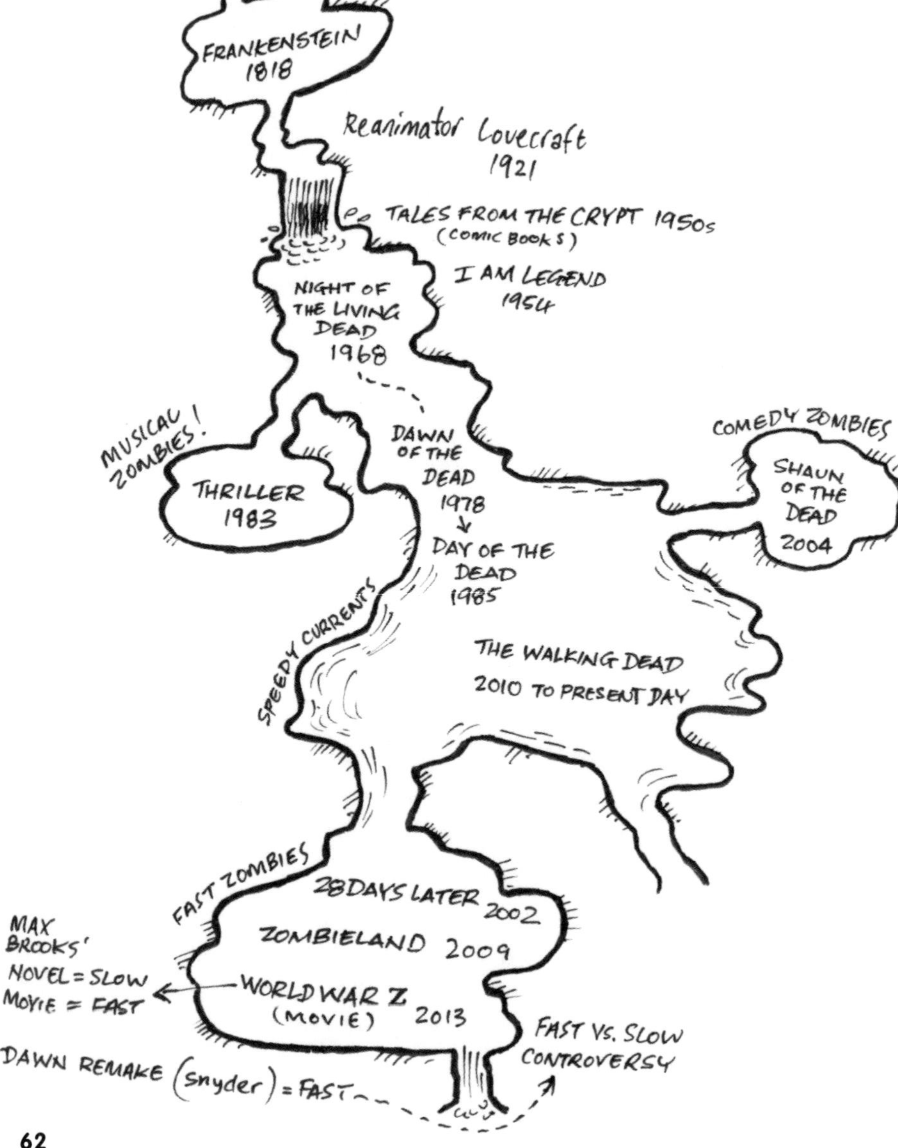

12. Systems Activity: The Bottom Left

As you move deeper into the collecting and shaping phase, it may start to feel as if there's almost too much to learn.

Sometimes the number of tasks you have to do can be overwhelming; lecturers and tutors are making demands from all angles and it's difficult to know where to start. The trouble with listing jobs is that a list doesn't allow you to see the bigger picture: you can't assess the progress of whole projects, you can only pick off small individual tasks.

Using a matrix or grid helps you to assess the status of entire subjects. And once you've got a good sense of how an entire subject is going, you can use your time much more effectively, targeting your energy where it's most needed.

Put every topic you need to master onto this grid:

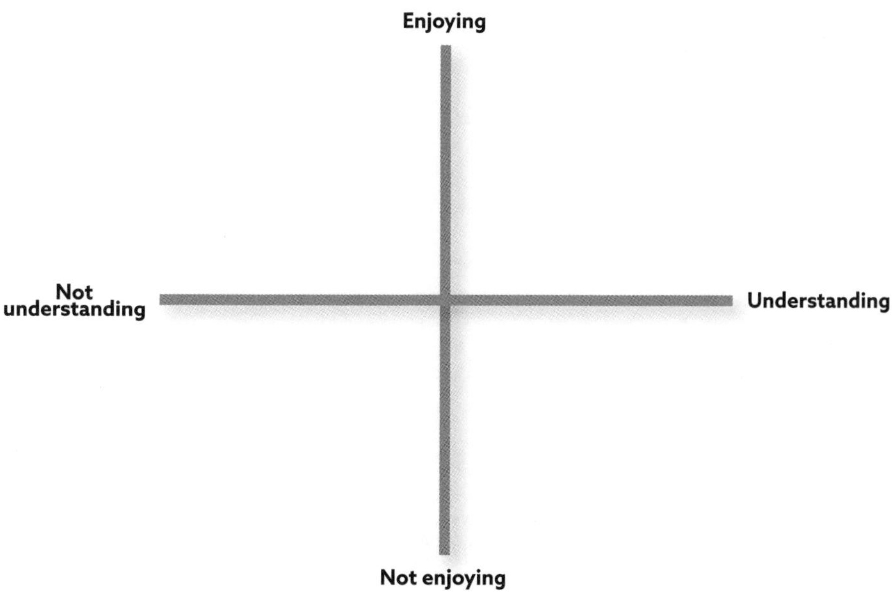

Once you've made these decisions and placed the topics as dots or crosses on the grid, make notes under each dot explaining the reasons why you've positioned it there. Then have a look at the projects in the bottom left of the grid.

The Terror of the Bottom Left!

Many of us subconsciously avoid projects in the bottom left because even the thought of them feels uncomfortable. But spending some time on these topics now can avoid a possible crisis later on.

Have a look at the projects closest to (or in) the bottom left quadrant. For each, make a note of:

* One task you could do that will push the dot further to the right:

  ....

  ....

  ....

  ....

* One task you could do that will push the dot further upwards:

  ....

  ....

  ....

  ....

It might be speaking to a lecturer, borrowing some missing work, designing a simple introduction to the topic based on your own research, speaking to a student who's better at it than you are or who has done it before, finishing a book on your reading list or making notes on a couple of academic papers.

Good prioritisation means knowing *why you're doing what you're doing*. Another problem with simple to-do lists is no matter how you prioritise your list, all the tasks still take up the same amount of physical space (a line of A4 paper) and so end up taking the same amount of mental space.

But not all tasks are equally important. Any tasks associated with projects that are currently in the top right quadrant, where you're understanding and enjoying the work, are a little less important than the tasks associated with the bottom left.

Have a look at the tasks you've got for topics in the top right quadrant. Is there any way you can complete these tasks more quickly and efficiently? Any small corners you can cut? Any favours you can call in or people you can ask for help? Your aim is to buy yourself some time by working super-efficiently on the projects that are currently going well.

Scribble some possible ideas here:

. . . .

. . . .

. . . .

. . . .

Now you've potentially saved yourself some time, note down below which task in the bottom left quadrant needs the most work:

. . . .

Use this saved time to get started on it now!

13. Systems Activity: Three Types of Attention

Everyone's day moves through phases, and you're probably no different – there are times when you're fired up and raring to go, there are times when your energy levels are just average and there are times when you feel your attention is low and your motivation dips.

These three phases happen to all of us during a working day. You're not unusual if you have low energy levels or can't concentrate; if you catch yourself looking around you and seeing others hard at work, remember they're no different to you – they're just in a different phase of their day.

Some people can predict when they're going to be feeling fired up (it might be the mornings, it might be after breakfast or after exercise) and when they're going to feel slower. Others haven't noticed a pattern, but once they pay attention they see one emerging. For others it's totally random.

Graham Allcott, founder of Think Productive (thinkproductive.co.uk), uses the following definitions for the three states:

1. **Proactive attention**
(fully focused, fired up, feeling fresh).
2. **Active attention**
(plugged in, ticking along nicely).
3. **Inactive attention**
(flagging, fried, foggy).

He argues that really successful people get work done in all three states. They don't give up when they're in state 3, they just switch tasks.

Make a list of all the tasks you've got on your plate at the moment. Now categorise them. Complex and challenging tasks go under 'proactive attention'. When you feel fully focused, fired up and fresh, you tackle those. Regular tasks go under 'active attention'. They're tasks to get on with when you feel you're ticking along nicely. Repetitive tasks that are pretty easy go under 'inactive attention'. When you're feeling fried or foggy, you switch to those tasks.

Proactive attention	Active attention	Inactive attention

Keep the list with you for a week or two. Whenever you're about to start working, check your energy levels. Sit still for a second and listen to your body. Decide which attention state you're in. Then review the list of tasks you've got to do that suit your attention level. If there are none in that column, find one from a neighbouring column and tackle it.

After a week or two, see whether you can observe patterns in your attention levels. One way to log your attention is to use colour coding. Use green for proactive attention, amber for active attention and red for inactive attention. You could use a grid that looks something like this:

	Mon	Tues	Wed	Thur	Fri	Sat	Sun
8-10am							
10am-12pm							
1-3pm							
3-5pm							
6-8pm							
8-10pm							

We've found that certain people move through predictable phases of attention. Some start the day full of energy, but dip slowly as the day goes on. Others respond to food – feeling more sluggish after lunch, for example. Others have worked out ways to jump into proactive attention before doing an important piece of work.

This last skill is really valuable. *If you can boost your attention, you can get more work done in less time*. Try experimenting with boosting attention. We've spoken to students who do the following:

* **Exercise just before work.** A run, a walk, a quick jog around the block or even an intense bout of star jumps!
* **Listen to music just before work.** A loud burst of motivating music with headphones on.

* **Use other pre-work rituals.** Some students talk about tidying their workspaces to get 'in the zone', having a hot shower, getting changed or engaging in a quick ten minute session of game-playing (bright, colourful puzzlers work much better than complex strategy or role playing games).

Use the space below to record your experiments and plans:

14. Systems Activity: Battling Information Overwhelm

Information overwhelm - the state of paralysis we feel when there's too much information to sort or filter - is a common occurrence when starting a new course or topic. References are made to journals or articles you haven't read; key names or studies are mentioned and you don't know what they are; and research makes it feel worse because there's so much out there.

Here are four ways to control the information flow and make things more manageable.

1. Strategic Ignorance

We love this simple approach for handling the fear you feel when you come across yet another new, weird and unexpected piece of information - *decide you're not going to learn about it yet.* Think: I'm deliberately shutting this out at the moment. Park it at the edge of your to-do list and forget it for now.

If other people know lots about it and keep mentioning it, rest easy. You've made a decision to deal with it later. Set a date for review - say, in a week's time - and then ask yourself some key questions:

- Does this thing seem crucial to my learning yet?
- Am I doing OK without it so far?
- Am I being actively mocked for not knowing about it?
- Have I got stuck without it?

If your answers to the above suggest you're doing OK without it, park it for another week.

2. Just in Time versus Just in Case

We all know a hoarder. They've got boxes of stuff they'll likely never use but they say, 'I'm keeping this *just in case* I need it one day.'

Then there are the just-in-time people. They haven't got what they need right now. Their rooms are uncluttered and calm. But if they're missing something really necessary, they can get it delivered tomorrow - *just in time*.

Information is the same. There's just-in-case information - that book you read that was full of ideas and information you never used or needed but it made you feel good to read it and take notes. And there's just-in-time information - that website you went through the week before a test that gave you two or three crucial ideas.

Review everything you're planning to read through and make a snap judgement. Move a load of stuff into the just-in-case pile, and start with the just-in-time stuff.

3. Three Points of Contact

We got this idea from studying rock climbing. The idea of three points of contact - that you should always have three points of connection between your body and the rock face - can be applied to reading too.

Read three sections of the text, rather than all of it, then make an assessment about whether you need to read the rest. Our favourite three points of contact with a textbook or article are:

1. **The introduction/abstract**: Does this look useful? If in doubt, skip to point 2.
2. **First third**: Skim-read until roughly the 30% point. How's it looking? If it's brilliant, go back and read the first third fully. If it's no good, ditch it. If you're not sure, skip to point 3.
3. **Conclusion**: Skip to the end for findings, summative remarks and distilled learning. Make a final judgement.

File under 'just in case' if you're not convinced, or switch it to 'just in time' if it's exactly what you're after.

4. The Podcast Lecture

Did you know that many scholars and experts summarise their new book in a specially designed short lecture delivered at a university or conference, and that this is often recorded?

We've taken advantage of this on many occasions when we've wanted to quickly read an important book to distil its wisdom. We've simply opened our podcast store, searched under the name of the writer and found a fifty minute lecture in which they summarise their book. The writer has spent hours choosing and preparing the most important aspects of their work for their audience. They've done the editing for you.

Thoughts, plans, ideas:

CHAPTER 4

Adapting, Testing and Performing

Key questions:
How can I recast this material so it's mine?
How do I create a working knowledge of it?
How do I demonstrate my mastery of this material and use it under pressure?
How do I prepare and practise?

Key elements of the VESPA model in this phase: effort, practice and attitude.

There's a big difference between information and knowledge. Before you enter the adapting, testing and performing phase, all you have is information. Lots of it, in note form. Turning that information into knowledge means using it practically to do this kind of stuff:

* Solve problems.
* Answer tricky questions.
* Generate solutions.
* Build arguments in essays.
* Critique points of view.
* Justify opinions.
* Evaluate outcomes.

In previous stages of education, most of what you needed to do was memorise information. The exam required you to regurgitate it. Not anymore. Now, you'll need to use the information you have to achieve things (it sounds obvious but a lot of students forget this). It takes practice to do this well.

Consider chess. Let's imagine you've never played before and you're challenged to a game by a friend. You don't prepare by reading 'How to Become a Grandmaster' and taking extensive notes. If you did, you might show up on game day with a huge amount of information - about the history of the game from its earliest origins to the artificial intelligence revolution, about its prominent players and their particular strategies, about all the possible opening moves or fiendish traps. But if this was all you had as you entered your high stakes match, you would be in trouble.

Instead, you would choose to actually *play chess*.

First, perhaps, you might find a fellow player who knew the game but was prepared to play a slowed down version with you. During play you would be looking for some key principles - how the game operates, what its component parts are, what seems to work and what doesn't. You would be asking questions and getting a sense of how it feels to play. (By the way, 'slow practice' is a technique used by musicians when practising tricky pieces.)

You might play two or three slow games as you figure out which piece does what and how the game tends to unfold; its beginning, middle and end. Once you reckon you've gathered enough information about the basics, you might then play a beginner - someone at a similar level to you. The information you've amassed from those slowed down early games can be applied as you try to execute a number of moves yourself, this time at normal speed.

You might play three or four times at normal speed, making as many mistakes as breakthroughs as you gradually work out what not to do as well as what seems to be successful. You're applying all the information you have and turning it into a working knowledge of the game (information + experience = knowledge).

So when you come up against that friend, it isn't the first time you've ever played chess. It might be the tenth or fifteenth. You've prepared as best you can. You might get a beating, but you've taken a few of those already and you know what it feels like. You perform pretty well and you discover a whole level of play above the one you're working at currently.

The same goes for your course. We believe that all practice falls into three stages:

1. Learn the content - gather and memorise all the information.
2. Develop a set of flexible skills through high stakes timed practice.
3. Seek feedback on performance and adjust accordingly.

When we polled our students (and those at two other schools just to check they weren't unusual), we found that students spent 80% of their time in stage 1, going over content. Around 15% of their time fell into stage 2, completing exam papers under timed conditions. The remaining 5% of their time was spent in stage 3, seeking feedback.

The balance was completely wrong: there was too much focus on gathering and memorising information in the content stage. The most effective students we've seen split their time reasonably equally across all three stages (we suggest about 40/30/30).

This, of course, requires *effort*. It's hard to go up against tricky questions over and over again, especially since the first few times you might perform relatively poorly. That's why we've included *attitude* in this section too. There will be setbacks and those nasty glitches will come calling, whispering that maybe you're not good enough. It's not true – and you will need to regularly remind yourself of that, and deal with those negative voices.

The tools in this chapter focus on effort, practice and attitude, giving you a range of approaches to try as you turn information into knowledge.

15. Effort Activity: The Three 'Hows' of Independent Work

We've worked with thousands of students who are great at designing revision. They create amazing revision and independent work plans that fill every minute of the day, but then just don't follow through on the plan.

It's something we've all done; if you have too, don't beat yourself up about it. Why do we procrastinate? Why do we avoid putting the effort in?

This might surprise you, but saying that you are going to do some 'revision' or 'independent work' is actually part of the problem. When you say that you are going to revise, the intended activity sounds vague and ambiguous. And when your brain thinks that you are about to do something that's vague and ambiguous, it will often start to come up with reasons why you shouldn't do it (which can be quite useful). It's not sure what you are going to be doing, or how, and your brain starts to get you thinking that it might not even work. Then you procrastinate.

So how do you get past this?

It's quite a simple strategy but we promise you it works. You have to get specific. Here's how. Before every revision or independent work session, you need to sit down and answer these three questions:

1 **How am I going to revise/work?** Here you have to be specific about the *how* (what strategy you are going to use) and also *what* you are going to revise. This means identifying specifically the topics you are going to focus on and the activities you're going to do to cover the work.

2 **How long am I going to revise/work for?** Be very clear about the time. If you are doing active revision this shouldn't be any longer than two hours. Remember to build in short (ten minute) breaks every forty minutes. Use Twenty-Five Minute Sprints (Activity 27) to help structure sessions and you will find it becomes even easier to beat procrastination.

3 **How will I know if I've made progress?** How are you going to test yourself? If you just sit for two hours passively reading your notes you will have no idea if you have made any progress, so you'll need to test yourself in some way. It might be a set of questions you answer, a mini-lecture you give to yourself or some short-answer questions you're going to do under timed conditions towards the end of the session.

You can get into the habit of doing this mentally, but, to start with, complete the table on page 79 before you begin every revision or independent work session.

Once you've done this a few times, you might start noticing that certain revision sessions feel easier than others. Watch out for sessions that feel too straightforward or too easy. Often they're the result of planning an activity that isn't very challenging and that is quite simple and often pretty boring to complete.

When you're working, try asking yourself, 'Would my strictest tutors let me get away with doing this for an hour?' If the answer is 'No,' it might be that you need to step up the challenge a little. In that way, you can get more done in less time.

How am I going to revise/work?	....
How long am I going to revise/work for?	....
How will I know if I've made progress?	....

16. Practice Activity: The Nine-Box Grid

An important step in owning information is recasting it – rewriting or reorganising your notes into something you've built yourself, something you've processed and created.

One way to do this is the nine-box grid. All you'll need is a sheet of A4 paper. Place the paper in front of you – orient it landscape – and fold it into thirds, like this:

Then, with it folded, do it again the other way so that when you open up you've got nine squares:

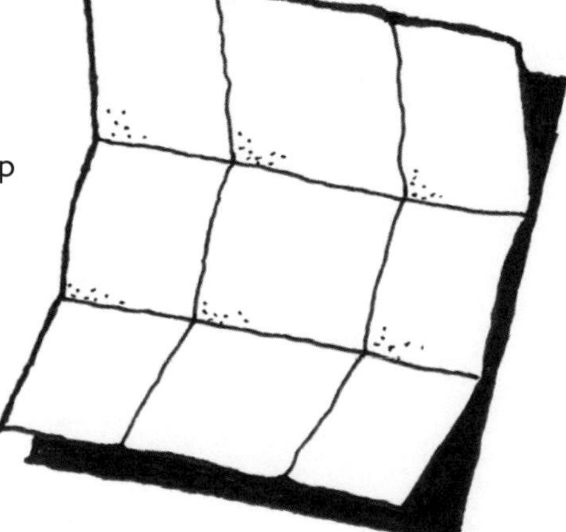

There are three steps to filling in the grid:

1 Your challenge is to summarise an entire topic in nine boxes. Begin by asking yourself: what are the nine key subsections? If I had to summarise this topic in nine bullet points, what would they be? How can I group similar material together? How can I connect things?

Subject or topic:

....

Nine possible topic areas:

1 ....

2 ....

3 ....

4 ....

5 ....

6 ....

7 ....

8 ....

9 ....

2 Once you've got the nine subsections, you need to find a way to summarise your notes using just the little boxes on the grid. You can't use any additional space, so go for diagrams, pictures, mind-maps or other graphic organisers to condense the information. Do what you have to, but get it all down in the nine little boxes. Then photograph it.

3 Now read through the whole grid and, on the other side, draw up a list of key concepts, ideas and vocabulary you're going to need to master. That's it. An entire topic on one sheet of paper.

Once you've got your nine-box grid, you're in a position where you really own the information. You own it because you've manipulated it, connected it and made fresh sense of it.

This process of recasting has a huge impact on your ability to keep hold of information and recall it.

17. Practice Activity: The Leitner Box

The Leitner Box, which was developed by the German scientist Sebastian Leitner, is a really effective, easy-to-develop practice and recall system. It's based on using flash cards to learn and then recall information, so this activity will need a whole bunch of subject-related flash cards. The cards are used as normal to record quick, easy-to-read bullet-pointed information about topics.

Leitner suggests that when we have a large amount of information to learn on flash cards, we have a tendency to gravitate towards the cards we already know and subconsciously avoid those we find difficult. To circumvent this, you create four subsections in your box (or four separate boxes):

* **Box 1.** Here you put items for frequent practice. This is the stuff you're not remembering well – it needs regular review and rereading because you're making mistakes when you practise recalling it or you don't know it at all. Around 40% of your time should be spent hammering the content of these cards. When you score a victory and fully recall a card, you move it down to box 2.
* **Box 2.** About 30% of your time is spent here. It's the stuff you've only just moved out of box 1 or that still trips you up or confuses you in any way. This material should be moving up (if you're not remembering it) or down (if you've nailed it) fairly regularly.
* **Box 3.** You spend 20% of your time here, and you nearly always get this stuff correct when you test yourself on it. You feel confident, even when the material is complex. However, if you dip in here and make any mistakes in recall at all, the card must be moved into box 2.

* **Box 4.** You begin with only a small number of cards here. This is the material you consider easy. You always get it right, so you only need to spend 10% of your time checking stuff in this box. However, and this is key, nothing ever leaves this box – because you know it so well. No matter how confident you feel, you still check it every now and again.

If you practise your recall in this way, you will find that you won't neglect information. You won't get caught by the 'familiarity trap' – the feeling that you know something so well that you never need to test yourself on it. Plus, you keep your focus where it needs to be: on the tough stuff that you keep forgetting.

Use the grid that follows to plan what information might belong in each box:

	Possible topics
Box 1: 40% of your time	....
	....

	Possible topics
Box 2: 30% of your time	....
Box 3: 20% of your time	....
Box 4: 10% of your time	....

If there's one quality we've seen that differentiates top performing students from others, it's the courage and determination to spend time focusing on weaknesses. This activity helps you to isolate where your attention needs to be. It may be uncomfortable, but it will make a huge difference to your levels of performance.

18. Attitude Activity: Failing Forwards

American journalist Dan Coyle (author of *The Talent Code* and *The Little Book of Talent*) argues that mistakes are information. He says that those who have become brilliant at something have got better at it more quickly because they have made a lot of mistakes and they have paid attention to their mistakes and drawn the learning out from them.

So, failure is important if we are ultimately going to succeed. There are, however, different attitudes to failure. Some students hate it and avoid it at all costs. It makes them feel embarrassed, humiliated and worthless. They hide their mistakes, don't complete tests or skip hard pieces of work so they can avoid failing. As a result they make slower progress.

Other students recognise the importance of failure. Your job is to try to become one of these people. John Maxwell puts it this way in his book *Failing Forward* (2012): some people fail backwards (the failure takes them in a backwards direction), whereas some people fail forwards (the failure accelerates their progress).

Have a look at the characteristics Maxwell associates with these different types of failing in the following table.

Failing backwards	Failing forwards
Blaming others.	Taking responsibility.
Repeating the same mistakes.	Learning from each mistake.
Expecting never to fail.	Knowing failure is part of the process.
Expecting to fail continually.	Maintaining a positive attitude.
Accepting tradition blindly.	Challenging outdated assumptions.

Failing backwards	Failing forwards
Being limited by past mistakes.	Taking new risks.
Thinking 'I am a failure'.	Believing something didn't work.
Withdrawing effort.	Persevering.

Now try to adapt your thinking so that it takes in the statements from the right-hand column.

- Take a recent failure and describe it in a paragraph. It might be a test or essay that went badly.
- Now look at your tutor's feedback. What are they picking out as areas of weakness? Make some notes about this, rephrasing their feedback in your own words.
- Finish by making a simple list: what are you going to do differently next time?

A recent failure:

....

....

....

....

The feedback I received:

....

....

....

....

Next time I need to:

. . . .

. . . .

. . . .

. . . .

. . . .

When you read Maxwell's descriptions of failing backwards, which of these are most like you? If you could pick one that you feel you need to stop doing, which one would it be? What are you going to do instead?

. . . .

. . . .

. . . .

. . . .

. . . .

CHAPTER 5

Flow and Feedback

Key questions:

Is there a level above where I'm at?

How do I access it?

Can I get some perspective and see what's going well and what isn't?

How come other people seem to be in the zone and I'm not?

Are there quicker ways to do this?

How do I fine-tune, tweak and iterate?

Key elements of the VESPA model in this phase: effort, practice and attitude.

Hungarian-American psychologist Mihaly Csikszentmihalyi first coined the term 'flow' in the 1960s, using it to describe a state of fully engaged, fluid and trance-like work. In an interview with John Geirland in 1996, Csikszentmihalyi talks of a feeling of complete immersion in an activity, so that 'nothing else seems to matter. The ego falls away. Time flies ... your whole being is involved, and you're using your skills to the utmost.'

The chances are we've all felt flow, perhaps while running, writing, painting or playing a game. A vast number of interviews with dancers, musicians, rock climbers, artists, surgeons, chess players and people from various disciplines and cultures convinced Csikszentmihalyi of the existence of flow states. Later in his career he turned his attention to the factors that contribute to the creation of these states.

Csikszentmihalyi suggested there were ten. For the sake of simplicity and practicality, the four that best apply to academic learning are:

1. **Clear goals, expectations and rules:** awareness of what makes a good performance, what the aims are, what will be judged (obtained from feedback, mark schemes or examples of other students' work).
2. **High levels of concentration and absorption** – so you need to be working in the right place!
3. **Immediate feedback** (not necessarily from a tutor): think qualitative feedback, a sense of whether things are going well or need adjustment.
4. **Balance between ability level and challenge:** the task is challenging but 'appropriately aligned with one's skill set and abilities' (Kotler, 2014, p. 30), which gives some sense of control over the situation, even if not complete and confident. In Csikszentmihalyi's words, 'flow involves meeting challenges and developing skills ... it leads to growth. It is an escape forwards from a current reality' (2003, p. 50).

Csikszentmihalyi concluded that flow states commonly arrived during the execution of 'painful, risky, difficult activities that stretched the person's capacity and involved an element of novelty and discovery' (1997, p. 110). In light of this, here are four questions to ask yourself:

1. **How comfortable does it feel as you work/revise/prepare/practise?** First think emotional and mental comfort – are you stretched or challenged by what you're doing? Then think physical comfort – where are you working? Lying on the sofa, on a bed, under a blanket, in an easy chair? We've found, on the whole, that notions of physical comfort vanish as learners approach flow. A spartan chair and table are all that's required.
2. **Do your study activities feel easy or comfortable?** What's the most difficult thing you've done in a recent session?
3. **What level of worry do you feel where you are?** How regularly are you failing at a challenge you've set or hitting obstacles when you work?
4. **Do you ever feel like time flies when you work?** Do you find yourself immersed in a problem or question? If so, when? Where? What are the triggers or patterns?

If you're too comfortable, it might explain why others are making more progress. They're working at harder tasks – and making the time count for more.

19. Practice Activity: Finding Flow

People seem capable of amazing work when they're in flow. They make swifter progress, they learn quickly, they stretch and challenge themselves, and they operate at a higher level. They seem to expend more mental effort and often feel pretty exhausted afterwards.

Lots of social scientists have studied and written about how to reach flow states. Two observations have emerged:

1. **There seems to be a connection between *flow* and *challenge*.** You can't reach flow doing something so easy it doesn't require your full concentration.
2. **There's a connection between *flow* and your *level of skill*.** You can't reach flow trying to attempt something that's way beyond your current capabilities.

But get the right balance of challenge and skill, and you begin to approach flow. One social scientist has produced a kind of emotional map to show us where flow is located. We've reproduced a modified version of it here.

Think of a swimming pool with three lanes like this:

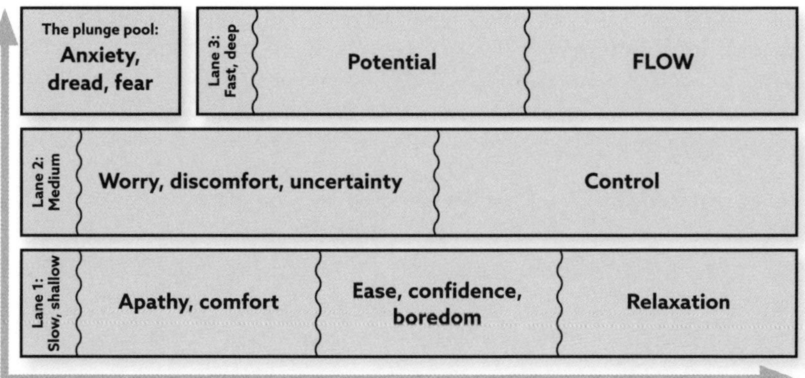

In lane 1 the water is warm. In other words, it's a nice, safe and comfortable place to be. The tasks here are low challenge and the work is easy. Even as your skill level increases, if you're in lane 1 you always feel relaxed.

In lane 2 the water is deeper and colder. It feels uncomfortable getting in if you're used to the warm water of lane 1. Swimmers move faster here – in other words, the work is harder. It often feels worrying, but stay long enough and you begin to feel in control.

In lane 3 the water is deep and cold. It's hard work here until you get used to it. Tasks are challenging and swimmers cut through the water quickly. Flow occurs in lane 3. There's no other way to get to it than by moving from lane 1, through lane 2 to lane 3.

The plunge pool – argh! Sometimes you try to move lanes too quickly, and end up losing your way and finding yourself in the plunge pool of anxiety. It's freezing in there! If you ever feel panic, if you ever feel overwhelmed or fearful, step back a little. Find a warmer, safer lane. Build your confidence there and then try to swap lanes again.

What Lane Are You In?

It could be that you're in different lanes for different parts of your course. So let's review your revision in just one subject area.

Subject: . . . .

How do you feel when you revise for this subject? Return to a memory from the last revision session you did. Now check that memory against the three lanes of the flow swimming pool. Your word might not be one of the words in the pool, but is it similar to one of them? Which lane do you think you're in at the moment? Record your thoughts here:

. . . .

. . . .

. . . .

Changing Lanes

Changing lanes is about increasing challenge. If you're interested in changing lanes, remember:

* You need to choose harder revision tasks to up your level of challenge and change lanes.
* This will start by feeling uncomfortable. Worry, stress or anxiety might be the emotions you begin to feel at first.
* But these feelings will disappear the longer you stay. Control or potential might be the states that replace it.

Let's finish with a list of revision activities you could be doing. To help you with this we have provided a set of strategies suggested by John Dunlosky from Kent State University in the United States. Dunlosky and his colleagues (2013) carried out a meta-study evaluating ten popular learning techniques and their effectiveness. (We've adjusted his language to make it more accessible in the table below.) How many have you used previously?

Technique	Always use	Sometimes use	Never use
Practice tests - adopting exam conditions, practising what is required in the time you're given.			
Spaced practice - scheduling practice tests and revision out over time; snacking instead of bingeing.			
Elaborative interrogation - explaining complex concepts and ideas to others - teaching someone else the material.			
Self-explanation - writing out explanations; clarifying how new information is linked to old information.			

Technique	Always use	Sometimes use	Never use
Interleaved practice - designing study that moves you from topic to topic, task to task and subject to subject rather than blocking out long sessions of the same activity.			
Summarising - writing out/ recording summaries of the information that is to be learned.			
Highlighting - pinpointing and highlighting key information as you read through your material.			
Mnemonics - using memorable words, phrases, acronyms or associations to boost recall.			
Text into image - attempting to turn information into images so as to better recall it.			
Rereading - setting out all your notes and course textbooks and reading through them again.			

Why This Order?

Dunlosky found the activities became less and less effective the further down this list they appear - the ones at the bottom had a low impact on learning and the ones at the top had a high impact. You can still do well using the low impact techniques, but you have to do a lot more work to make it stick. And it takes longer. You can make your study more effective by pushing yourself up the list. Some of the activities towards the top are hard work - but they have a big impact.

Using the table on page 96, try placing these strategies first, and then add your own - there will be plenty you're doing that isn't on Dunlosky's list. If the strategy seems easy and comfortable, put it in lane 1. If it makes you feel uncomfortable or slightly worried, put it in lane 2. If the thought of it makes you feel fear and dread, put it in lane 3.

Lane	Indicative states	Activity
1	Apathy, comfort, ease, confidence, boredom, relaxation	* .... * .... * .... * .... * ....
2	Worry, discomfort, uncertainty, control	* .... * .... * .... * .... * ....
3	Potential, flow	* .... * .... * .... * .... * ....

Next time you're feeling like progress is slow and you're comfortable and bored, you know it's time to change lanes. Choose an activity from a deeper, colder lane of the pool!

20. Practice Activity: K-SPA

Chartered psychologist and university lecturer Alison Price is interested in the psychology of successful people. Having spent time researching and interviewing, she proposes an interesting model for the types of preparation people do before a learning breakthrough. These barrier busting breakthroughs don't come overnight, Price argues – they're the result of careful planning, preparation and determined action.

But faced with a problem, it's normal to sometimes feel gloomy and defeated. How do we get past this? Where should we start? What should we do next?

We've adapted Price's work to create the K-SPA model. It suggests four things you should focus on in order to break through a barrier:

K **Knowledge.** Things you need to *know more about* in order to break down the barrier.

S **Shopping.** Things it would be *useful to have* in order to break down the barrier.

P **Practising.** Things you *need to be better at* in order to break down the barrier.

A **Action.** Things you could *do right now* in order to break down the barrier.

First, begin by identifying your barrier. You're capable of blasting it away in the next few weeks. Choose a barrier that is preventing you from moving forward.

The problem or barrier:

....

....

Now use the four headings below to begin brainstorming solutions. Once you've got a whole bunch under each heading, your task is to choose the one that will have the highest impact – and commit to it. You should end up with four doable actions that you can now sequence.

Knowledge	Possible areas for research and learning: * .... * .... * ....
	The one thing I'll study:
Shopping	Possible purchases: * .... * .... * ....
	The one thing I'll buy:
Practising	Possible areas for practice: * .... * .... * ....
	The one thing I'll practise:
Action	Possible actions I could take straight away: * .... * .... * ....
	The one thing I'll do now:

The important thing here is to commit to the four actions. To maximise your chances of success, choose actions you know you can execute, and schedule them so you know when you should be taking that action.

If you're stuck or it didn't work, return to your list of possible actions and choose another. This trick works because it gives you four simple things to do. Remember, you don't need to do them in order.

Or, try this. Rank your four actions from the hardest to do to the easiest to do. Now complete them in the following order:

Make action 1 the second easiest.

Action 1: ....

By when: ....

Make action 2 the third easiest.

Action 2: ....

By when: ....

Now give yourself a reward. You've done two of your four steps. A break is in order!

Make action 3 the easiest action to do.

Action 3: ....

By when: ....

Finish with action 4 – the hardest of the lot.

Action 4: ....

By when: ....

Play with the order of the actions if you want – find the sequence that best suits your temperament or state of mind. Hopefully Price's technique will help you to break down barriers and get some forward momentum!

21. Attitude Activity: The Problem Solving Cycle

This activity is based on the work of David Kolb from the University of Leicester. Kolb's work suggests that we learn best through experience – through doing. If we take action and attempt a challenge (therefore experiencing something rather than just reading or thinking about it), our awareness, understanding and mastery increases. Kolb proposes that 'experiential learning', as he calls it, passes through four phases (see McLeod, 2017).

When we first saw Kolb's work, his four phases were presented as a framework for problem solving. It worked really well for us and we became hooked. We'll share what we learned with you here. You'll need to set aside thirty minutes to start with.

First, choose a problem you're battling with or a barrier you're facing. It might be to do with study habits, current performance, levels of energy or a subject-specific issue.

The problem or barrier:

. . . .

The result of the problem:

. . . .

Now, using the grid on page 102, break down the problem into the four stages of Kolb's problem solving cycle – making use of the guidance provided on page 101 to inform you on how best to approach each stage.

1. EXPLORE THE PROBLEM

Key question: 'What is currently happening?'

Stay here for ten minutes, assessing *the exact situation you are in*. Do not use judgemental or emotional language ('terrible', 'crap', nightmare'). Use facts and figures ('I'm on a grade E', 'My motivation is very low'). Dredge up every last bit of evidence you can find - grades, test scores, attendance, levels of effort and energy, feedback. Describe only - do not use 'because' yet; avoid justifying anything. Calmly list everything about your current situation.

2. ANALYSE THE PROBLEM

Key question: 'Why is it happening?'

Stay here for ten minutes. List every single reason *why the problem is happening*. Make your list as long as possible, exploring yourself and your own actions, your attitudes and beliefs, the influence of those around you, your tutorials, seminars, work materials, the impact of external events, the impact of lecturers, tutors and so on.

Calmly list everything, making sure nothing is missed. Don't bother yourself with solutions yet. Take your time.

3. DECIDE A COURSE OF ACTION

Key question: 'What are my options?'

Stay here for ten minutes. Look back at what is happening and why. *Only focus on the things you can solve*. Calmly set aside anything outside your control. Sift through your analysis of the problem and begin listing things you could do. Be uncritical; ignore the part of your brain saying, 'That's a terrible idea!' or 'How could that work? It's ridiculous!' and continue to list courses of action. Start with 'I could ...' and go from there. When you're stuck, bring to mind everyone who could help - tutors, mentors, parents, family, friends.

When you've completed your list, choose your favourite three, then your top option.

4. EXPERIMENT WITH A COURSE OF ACTION

Key question: 'How did it go, and what have I learned?'

You'll be in this phase for a week. Try out your chosen adjustment. As you go along, get a sense of how it is working. Persist with it, thinking about its impact on your learning.

Then assess it at the end of the period. Discard, repeat or modify.

4. EXPERIMENT WITH A COURSE OF ACTION	1. EXPLORE THE PROBLEM
Key question: 'How did it go, and what have I learned?'	**Key question:** 'What is currently happening?'
3. DECIDE A COURSE OF ACTION	**2. ANALYSE THE PROBLEM**
Key question: 'What are my options?'	**Key question:** 'Why is it happening?'

Each of us apparently has a preference for one of these stages and we might have a tendency to linger in it or even stay there for as long as possible. We all know someone who endlessly talks about a problem without ever doing anything about it (as Independent Thinking founder Ian Gilbert says, 'Creativity starts with "If only …" Mediocrity ends with it' (2014, p. 57)). That person might feel most comfortable in stage 1 or 2 – describing or analysing the problem.

If this is you, it's well worth keeping an eye out for the kind of reasons you specify. External justification is the tendency to blame everything on issues beyond our control. In contrast, by taking responsibility for your problems and internally justifying, you're much more likely to generate solutions.

Internal justifications	**External justifications**
I guess I'm not really concentrating.	The lectures are really dull.
I haven't been reading widely from my list.	The topics are impossible.
I don't get up early enough.	It's a nightmare getting in. Public transport is terrible.
I don't ask enough questions to clarify my understanding.	Tutorials go too quickly. I can't keep up.

For the cycle to work, stay in each quadrant for a good period of time, getting the most out of each stage.

Kolb's approach to problem solving is called root cause analysis – that is, a close examination of why a problem is occurring and where it's growing from. But there are other methods to solving problems.

Take a look at the following techniques and see if any of them might help you to generate some possible solutions. There's space under each heading for you to scribble some initial ideas.

1 **Breaking down.** One big problem might look too much to handle, but every big problem is composed of smaller problems. With this approach, you identify one or two smaller issues, and try to fix those first.

2 **OODA.** Designed by a US Air Force colonel called John Boyd, this stands for *observe*, *orient*, *decide* and *act*. It's a simple four-step problem solving approach that begins with closely studying a problem before choosing a way forward.

3 **Prove it.** This technique involves trying to prove that the problem is impossible to solve. Gather as much evidence as you can to demonstrate there's no way out. Wherever you can't prove that it's unsolvable, make a note of why – the possible solutions may well lie there.

We were once told about 'the three B's of creativity', an idea sometimes attributed to the Austrian-British philosopher Ludwig Wittgenstein (according to Schank et al., 2010, p. 37). Creative problem solving often occurs when we least expect it to. The B's in question are *bed* (i.e. we problem solve subconsciously when we take a nap), *bath* (when we deliberately relax and switch off) and *bus* (when we travel, move or exercise). So if you're stuck, you could try one of these!

Don't feel you need to stay loyal to one of the approaches described above - a combination might work for you. Whatever you try, the solutions you come up with will be better ones as a result.

22. Attitude Activity: Managing Reactions to Feedback

Our responses to getting feedback can vary considerably. Some people are hungry for feedback and want to know how they can improve; others avoid feedback like the plague and take it personally. But if you want to get better at something, you're going to have to get comfortable with feedback. Steve Bull, in his brilliant book *The Game Plan* (2006, p. 125), has developed an acronym, SADRAA, to help you with the process. He suggests that when you get feedback you might not be happy with, you should work through three stages: the red zone, the blue zone and the green zone.

The table that follows explains the zones. Low performing students can sometimes get caught up in the red zone, and some might never leave. You might know people like this! It's fine to have these initial emotions, of course, but then you must push through to the next two stages.

THE RED ZONE Emotions	**S**hock	Wow – I did not expect that! I'm really surprised by those comments.
	Anger	How dare they say that! That tutor has never liked me. Wait till I get my own back.
	Denial	I'm not like that at all. That's totally wrong.

THE BLUE ZONE Thinking	**R**ationalisation	OK, maybe it seems true from their perspective. But the reason they think that is because they don't know what kind of pressure I'm under. Anyway, that's the way I am and why should I change? And even if I wanted to, how could I?
THE GREEN ZONE Behaviour	**A**cceptance	OK, maybe I need to change something. Maybe I could look at a few different ways of doing things to see if they improve matters.
	Action	Right, what do I need to do?

The next time you get some feedback that you might not be happy with, use the table on page 108 to either record your own thoughts or check in with your emotional response to the criticism and assess which zone you're in. Then look ahead to the next zone and see what kind of thoughts you might try to have in order to move yourself through the process more quickly. Ultimately, you'll be much happier if you avoid getting stuck in the red or blue zone!

It might be tricky to get to the green zone, so feel free to leave it for a day or so – maybe longer – before completing the final box or considering the ideas you see there.

The zones	Your thoughts
The red zone Emotions	
The blue zone Thinking	
The green zone Behaviour	

One way to fully understand Bull's model is to observe other people responding to feedback. Watch for feedback after a sporting fixture and see how the players react. Watch out for how your parents describe receiving feedback, or even your tutors. Most of all, watch for how your friends talk about feedback. If you're surrounded by people who can't take feedback, it makes it harder to learn how to handle it well.

Writer and artist Austin Kleon warns us to make sure we have positive friends. He calls negative friends 'vampires'. Kleon advises that 'if, after hanging out with someone you feel worn out and depleted, that person is a vampire. If, after hanging out with someone you still feel full of energy, that person is not a vampire' (2014, p. 129).

Think about the five people you spend most time with and ask yourself five questions about them:

1. Are they positive people?

   ....

   ....

2. Do they enjoy their lives?

   ....

   ....

3. Are they a good influence?

   ....

   ....

4. Have they helped you through problems?

   ....

   ....

5. Do they make you feel good about yourself, and about life?

   ....

   ....

If you answer 'no' to any of these questions, you might want to reconsider who you spend your time with!

CHAPTER 6

Dealing with the Dip

Key questions:
It's all gone pear-shaped.
How do I get out of this?
Is this just me?
Why am I even bothering?
Are there systems to help me get through these difficult times?

Key elements of the VESPA model in this phase: vision, effort and attitude.

> *Pain + Reflection = Progress*
>
> **Dalio (2017), p. 549**

Do you remember how excited you were when you received the letter to let you know that you'd been accepted onto your course? You were probably delighted – at least for a while. We've seen thousands of students go crazy on results day, discovering that they've made it onto a university course that they've been thinking about for years. Some students celebrate for weeks.

Five months pass by, and you might be wondering why you even went to college or university. You hate it! Don't worry. You've just hit 'the dip'. It happens to nearly every student we've ever worked with.

Many writers and thinkers have analysed the dip and why it happens. Here are five different perspectives.

1. The Dip

Entrepreneur Seth Godin puts it this way. 'At the beginning, when you first start something, it's fun. Over the next few days and weeks the rapid learning you experience keeps going.' Then comes the dip. 'The Dip,' Godin explains, 'is the long slog between starting and mastery' (2007, pp. 17–18). If there was no dip, everyone would be a brilliant musician, a world-class skier or a surfing guru. The reason they aren't is that, according to Godin, most of them quit in the dip.

Figure 6.1. The Dip

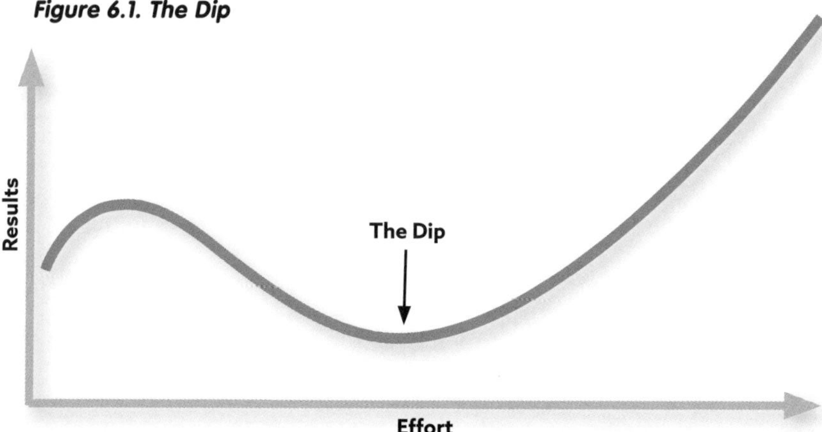

2. The Project Plateau

Author and investor Scott Belsky's concept of the project plateau is similar. 'The project plateau,' he says, 'is littered with the carcases of dead ideas that have never happened. What do we do? We escape this project plateau with a new idea.' According to Belsky, when we reach a plateau, our tendency is to ditch the hard project and start something new so we can return to that excited feeling of beginning something. 'And this is why,' he explains, 'there are more half-written novels in the world than there are novels' (see Popova, 2011).

3. The Change Curve

The Change Curve was developed in the 1960s by psychologist Elisabeth Kübler-Ross to explain the phases people go through during the grieving process. Nowadays, the curve is used to help people understand their reactions to significant change in their lives.

Kübler-Ross discusses the tendency of some people to get stuck in the 'emotional fog', slowing their psychological recovery. Similarly, as learners, we might feel it is impossible to adjust to our new situation. We're caught in the dip.

Figure 6.2. The Change Curve

4. The Wall

The wall is a term specific to endurance sports, often marathon running, and describes the point, usually at about 20 miles, when the runner experiences sudden fatigue and hopelessness. Aylin Woodward, writing in the *New Scientist* in 2018, describes it this way, 'Those who have been through it describe the experience as a sudden onset of debilitating fatigue and loss of energy that happens during the race's latter half.' She goes on, 'Formerly speedy runners slow to a shuffle ... and a racer swiftly switches from a desire to finish in a certain time to a yearning to just finish at all.'

5. The Trough of Sorrow

Paul Graham talks about 'The Process' most people go through with any project, whether it's starting a course or setting up a new business.* It's important to remember that there are usually two easy bits to any project – the start and the finish! We begin most projects with some excitement. The majority of students love it when they first start sixth form or university. It's a new environment, with new people and with new things to learn.

But after a while the novelty wears off. It's a bit like the excitement you feel when you get a new phone. Two months later and you're already looking at the new releases, wishing you had one of those instead. As you start any course, the work tends to get harder and the deadlines for exams or coursework loom.

The next stage is what Graham calls the 'trough of sorrow'. This dip can be a cold, harsh place. Negative thoughts dominate your thinking, and you can struggle to see any light at the end of the tunnel.

---

* 'The Process' was originally called 'The Startup Curve'. It was designed by Paul Graham of Y Combinator and appears on the *Business Insider* website: http://www.businessinsider.com/chart-of-the-day-the-startup-curve-2012-3?IR=T.

Figure 6.3: The Process

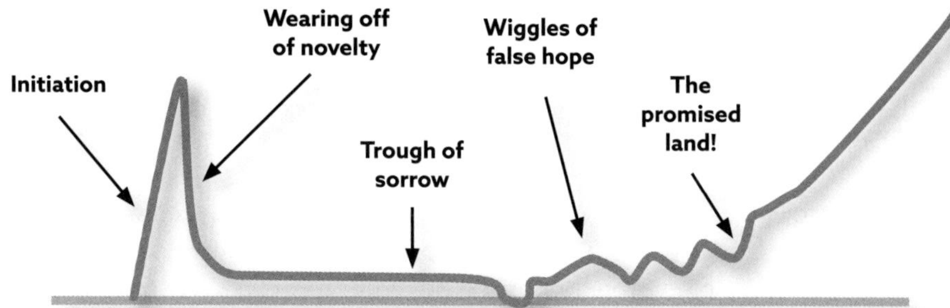

Don't deny the dip! There's no point in pretending this isn't going to happen to you. Better to accept the inevitability of the dip, and remind yourself that the dip is where you will be assailed by the five glitches. They will come from inside you, manifesting as negative self-talk. But don't despair. There's always a path forward; you just need a plan and some simple tools to get you there.

The first two activities in this chapter will help you to face the dip objectively and review what's happening. Read them both and then pick one to have a go at ...

23. Vision Activity: Dalio's Process

Ray Dalio is an American billionaire investor. As of January 2018, he was one of the world's 100 wealthiest people. He's now turned his attention to helping other people be the best they can be. In his book, *Principles* (2018), he suggests a five-step process to help you get out of the dip.

Step 1: Know Your Goals and Run After Them!

When you're deep in the dip you sometimes have to remind yourself of your why. We dealt with this in Chapter 1. At some point you really wanted to be where you are now. It might not feel like it at the moment, but you were probably excited to start your course.

Remind yourself of the why here.

I started this course because:

....

....

Step 2: Visualise the Problems That Stand in Your Way

Now you've reminded yourself of your goals, you have to figure out what the barriers to your progress are. In his book *Good to Great* (2001), Jim Collins describes facing brutal truths. You can't bury your head in the sand – it's time to face facts.

To help you do this, it's worth doing an activity called zones of control. You'll need some sticky notes for this one.

Using one sticky note at a time, write down all the obstacles you can think of. Just keep writing and thinking of as many difficulties as you can. Some will be internal, others external. Grab them all.

The next step is to place them on an enlarged version of the zones of control diagram below. Take each sticky note and ask yourself, how much control do I have over this? Is it no control (there is nothing you can do about it – e.g. external factors such as ill health or family problems)? Or could you somehow influence the obstacle (it might appear to be outside your control but there are some things you could do to make it better)? Finally, is this something that is within your control (e.g. you might not have been working hard enough but you know there aren't really any excuses for this)?

Use the diagram below – an adaptation of the work of Stephen Covey (1989) – to decide which of your problems lie in your 'zone of control'. These are the ones you can quickly do something about. Then consider which ones lie in your 'zone of influence'. Here, you'll be able to take steps towards alleviating the problem, though you might need to call in some favours or involve others. Finally, place what's left in the 'zone of no control'. Like the weather on a wedding day, we've no control over what happens. Whatever these issues are, we have to let them go and stop giving them our time and mental energy.

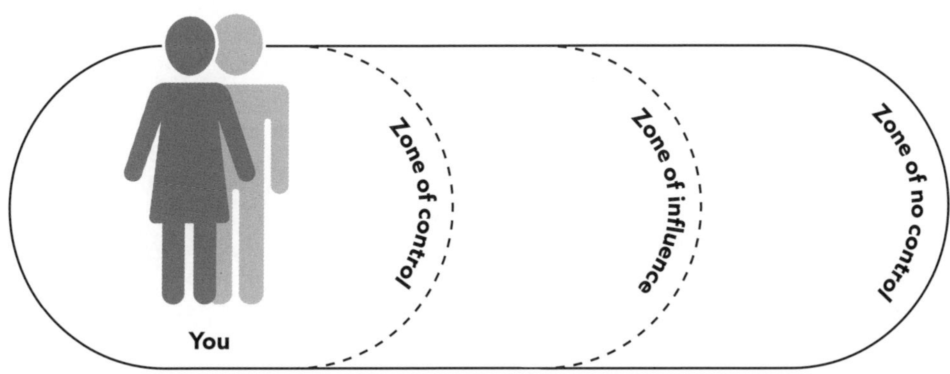

When you've decided where to place your sticky notes, it's often useful to share your thoughts with another person, if you feel comfortable doing so. Sometimes we can believe we have no control when in fact we do. Getting a different perspective can help with this. Some things you just can't control, so you have to let them go. It's the stuff you *can* influence and the things within your control that we need to investigate a little further.

Step 3: Diagnose the Problems to Get At Their Root Causes

Now you need to go deep and drill down into the problem. The 'five whys', developed by Sakichi Toyoda at Toyota to fine-tune the company's manufacturing production system, is a fantastic tool to get to the bottom of any problem.

Take one of your sticky notes - one of the factors that you can control - and then interrogate it five times by asking 'why'. This is harder than it sounds, so have a look at these examples:

I'm not attending lectures and seminars.

Why?

Because I'm staying in bed until late in the morning.

Why?

Because I don't feel motivated to go in.

Why?

Because I'm not enjoying it.

Why?

Because I'm not sure this exact course is the right one for me anymore.

Why?

Because it's too theoretical and doesn't allow me to do the practical work I really want to do.

By the fifth why you've usually got down to the real issue – something you can deal with and take some action to fix. This student needs to speak to their tutor about, for example, adjusting their course, swapping to a slightly different course in year two or joining a more practical class.

Don't feel you necessarily have to ask why five times. You might stop before the fifth why. Notice how the line of interrogation above concludes – it can't go any further. The final 'because' (because the course is too theoretical) is out of the student's control. It's an external factor. If we ask why again, all we get is, 'They designed it that way because they wanted to.' We're not analysing controllables anymore, so it's time to stop.

Here's a shorter example:

I feel demotivated and I'm losing interest in this class.

Why?

My work isn't any good.

Why?

Well, I work hard at it. (Thinks ...) My feedback says I need to evaluate studies in more detail.

Why?

Obviously the tutor mentioned it because she thinks it's a weakness.

Here we're done after three whys – the line of questioning leaves us with the tutor's feedback. That's an external factor. (Ask another why and all we get is, 'I don't know. She just does.') We also have the beginnings of a possible solution – finding out what good evaluation looks like by checking out someone else's work.

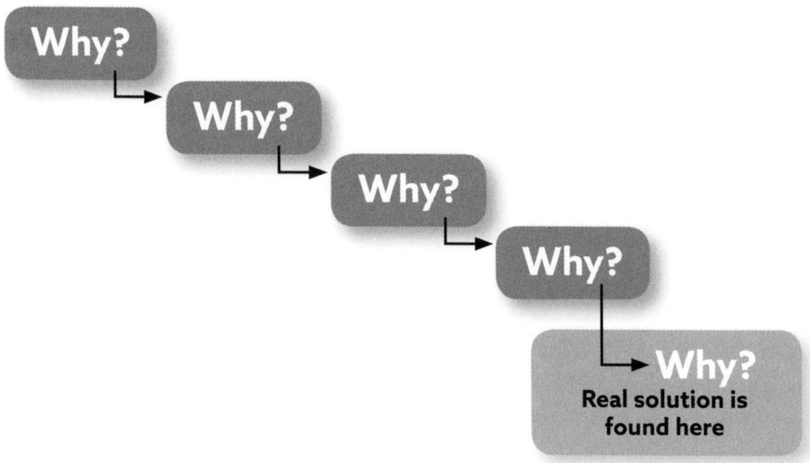

One other thing: what happens if you ask why and two or three possible answers suggest themselves? Record them all, then follow each one. Some will be dead ends, while others may converge on the same issue the deeper you go.

Remember: *stop when the issue becomes an external one beyond your control.* That's often where you need to begin considering solutions. Speaking of which ...

Step 4: Design a Plan to Eliminate the Problems

Next you need a plan. Deciding where you are going to focus your efforts often is the most important part of any plan. To help you with this you need the Eisenhower Matrix.

This model was supposedly developed by former US president Dwight Eisenhower – he was considered a master of time management, always getting everything done by the deadline. Eisenhower apparently put all his tasks into one of four boxes on the matrix. He then dealt with the ones that were urgent and important. Only when all the tasks in this box were complete did he move on to the remaining jobs.

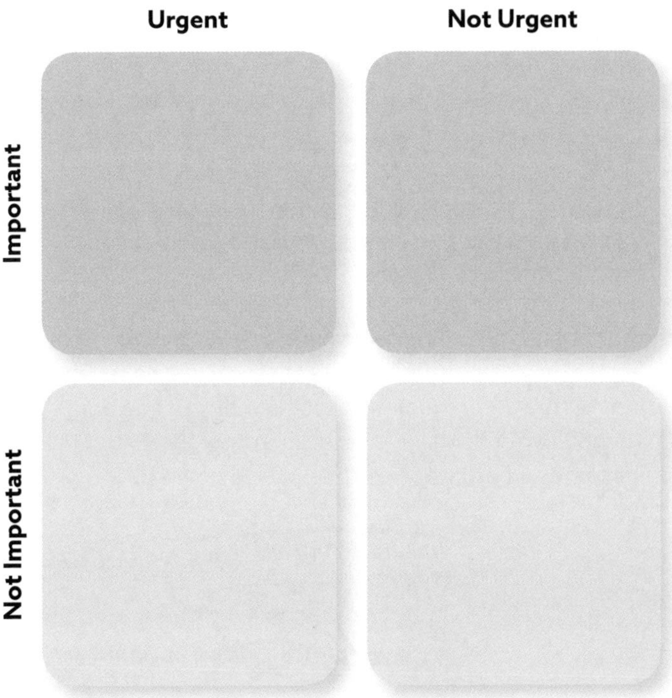

List absolutely everything you have to do in the matrix, including all the ideas that have come from step 3. You might have twenty or thirty things to do, from finishing work to sending emails, setting up meetings or revising for tests. Decide in which quadrant each task belongs.

You know now where you need to focus your efforts. You just need to carry out your plan.

Step 5: Execute Your Plan

Now is the time to take action! You need a bit of courage for this – there are going to be jobs you're dreading. If you do feel some trepidation, consider the cost of doing nothing. Deciding not to take action has repercussions too. What will happen if you just let this fester? Spend some time thinking this through, and you might find that action – uncomfortable as it is – beats doing nothing.

24. Effort Activity: The Four Disciplines of Execution

One of the most common realisations students face when they're in the dip is that they've put themselves there by not doing enough work. The instant gratification monkey takes hold of you and drags you off in every direction but towards your academic work. Even tidying your kitchen becomes a better option than sitting down to study.

So how do you ditch the monkey and get stuff done? Chris McChesney, Sean Covey and Jim Huling have a simple four-step plan that will help you start working. It's called the four disciplines of execution.

Discipline 1: Keep Your Focus Narrow

In their book *The 4 Disciplines of Execution* (2012), the authors argue that the more we focus on, the less we actually accomplish. So you need to focus on less to get more done. We know this sounds counterintuitive, but if you want to avoid the gratification monkey you need to be very specific about what you want to achieve.

Consider these two examples:

Unspecific:

'I've got masses to do. Loads of revision, missing notes and hours of reading to catch up on.'

Result: paralysis

Specific:

'I need to do fifty minutes of reading per day and write 800 words per day for a week to catch up.'

Result: action

By refining your goals, your focus improves – and, suddenly, previously impossible tasks seem much more doable.

Discipline 2. Act on Leading Indicators

The concept of leading and lagging indicators is explained in the diagram below:

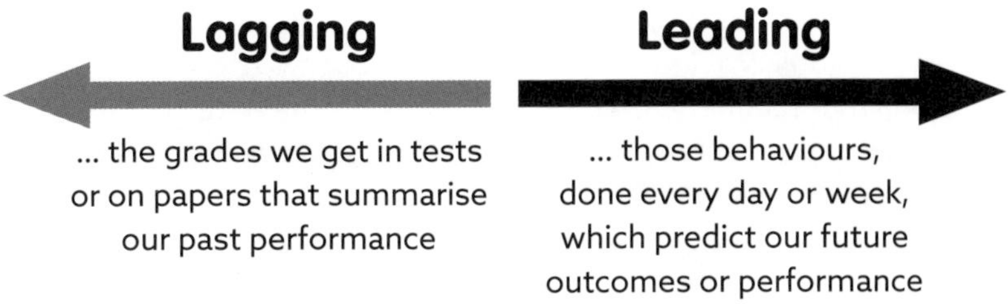

Lagging ←	→ **Leading**
... the grades we get in tests or on papers that summarise our past performance	... those behaviours, done every day or week, which predict our future outcomes or performance

We think that this is one of the most important aspects of getting out of the dip. Most people focus on *lagging* indicators when they are trying to achieve something. A lagging indicator tells you what past performance has been like – for example, the grade you achieved on a piece of work last term. It summarises the quality of the two weeks you spent putting the work together.

A *leading* indicator gives you an idea of what's going to happen as a result of your current behaviour. It tells you whether you are going to hit your target. For example, if you were completing a 5,000 word essay, but your current daily word count is 50, we have a leading indicator that tells us you aren't going to make it. But you might decide to write 500 words a day, so that you hit your deadline on time.

What leading indicators could you set yourself? You might use hours per day of revision, chapters read, papers read and annotated, studies summarised or number of words written. Establish your own leading indicators and you can get through the dip one day at a time.

Discipline 3: Keep a Compelling Scoreboard

There's a saying in management: what gets measured gets managed. This is why keeping a scoreboard is a key part of the dip rescue process. You might use something as simple as a calendar. Every time you complete your 500 words, your two hours of revision, your reading and so on, you cross off the date. You'll find that once you have three, four or five crosses in a row, you won't want to break the pattern.

Sunday	Monday	Tuesday	Wednesday	Thursday	Friday	Saturday
		~~1~~	~~2~~	~~3~~	~~4~~	~~5~~
~~6~~	~~7~~	~~8~~	~~9~~	~~10~~	11	12
13	14	15	16	17	18	19
20	21	22	23	24	25	26
27	28	29	30	31		

Discipline 4: Create a Cadence of Accountability

A *what*? Most people execute more consistently when they are being held to account. You need to choose someone or something that acts as a motivator and holds you to account. Your first thought might be a parent, tutor or friend. But not everyone can rely on that kind of accountability.

Tim Ferriss, the author of *The 4-Hour Work Week* and *Tribe of Mentors*, has an unusual accountability system. He struggled for years with procrastination before hitting upon it. It's pretty extreme – one of those times when you think, if this is the solution, how bad was the problem?! Let's consider it here:

1. **Step 1:** He gives a friend a sum of money – not enough to make him broke if he lost it, but enough that a loss would be painful.
2. **Step 2:** He then makes a promise to the friend that he will complete X by a given time. Ferriss has used this strategy when writing books, committing himself to writing a certain number of words each day.
3. **Step 3:** If he doesn't hit the target, it is his friend's responsibility to hold him to account. If he doesn't do what he committed to do, all the money is donated to a specific cause. (You might think you could live with that, but Ferriss makes sure that the cause is something he really doesn't agree with and goes against all his values!)

25. Attitude Activity: Beating Procrastination

Dr Neil Fiore has written what many consider to be the key text on procrastination – *The Now Habit*. The section that follows is an exploration and adaptation of his work. For the original, check out his super-helpful book. It's short, clear and practical.

Fiore argues that we procrastinate because of our status relationship with the work we face. Imagine a see-saw with you on one end and the task on the other. Here, the task is elevated in status and becomes bigger than the student:

How do we create this situation? It works like any see-saw – we lower ourselves so the task rises above us. It becomes a dominant monster in our minds. Fiore describes how, when you do this, you change an ordinary task – one you are capable of completing well – into 'a test of your worth, proof that you are acceptable, or a test of whether you will be successful and happy or a failure and miserable' (2007, pp. 49–50).

Our response to this threat is procrastination. We avoid the task until the very last moment, before reluctantly battling it. We begin to

dread similar tasks. Fiore argues that *we* are responsible for lowering ourselves and raising the status and importance of the task. We turn ordinary assignments into tests of self-worth.

How? We do it through our own self-talk – our glitches. In his 1998 book *How to Stubbornly Refuse to Make Yourself Miserable About Anything (Yes, Anything!)*, American psychologist Albert Ellis looked at irrational and negative thinking experienced by people in times of stress. He called this 'crooked thinking'.

His work can be applied directly to students in stressful situations. He indentifies six specific types of crooked thinking. Three are associated with lowering your status and thinking of assignments as tests of self-worth:

1. **Catastrophe thinking:** 'If this goes wrong, it'll be a total nightmare.'
2. **Stopper thinking:** 'I'm useless. I can't do this. I'm bound to screw up. What's the point in starting?'
3. **Illogical thinking:** 'If this bad thing happens, this one will surely follow ...'

This might be you. Or not – there's a second way things can pan out:

Here, the student raises themselves above the assignment. A little self-confidence can be a good thing – but in this extreme position, the result is the same as before: procrastination. The student thinks the task is pointless, a waste of time and an unnecessary additional burden on their week. Fiore puts it this way: 'you delay starting out of a need to assert your independence and to resist ... [doing] even a simple task' (2007, p. 48).

Ellis describes three types of crooked thinking typical in this situation:

1. **'Not fair' thinking:** 'I shouldn't have to do this. The whole thing seems pointless. They don't have to do this on other courses.'
2. **Blaming thinking:** 'It's the lecturer's fault. This task is badly designed. It's the course leader's fault. It's everyone's fault except mine.'
3. **Overgeneralising:** 'This always happens to me. I end up doing pointless stuff. The whole organisation is rubbish. I'm not participating.'

So what's the answer? It's this:

To see the assignment or task for what it is. To face it head-on as an equal. A phrase we've heard students repeating in these situations is: 'Get it done. Submit. Move on.'

There's a great metaphor for expressing this balance – having a mind like water. Here's David Allan in his productivity book *Getting Things Done*: 'Imagine throwing a pebble into a still pond. How does the water respond? The answer is, totally appropriately to the force and mass of the input ... It doesn't overreact or underreact.' He adds, 'Most people give either more or less attention to things than they deserve, simply because they don't operate with a "mind like water".'*

Fiore suggests imagining that your task is to walk along a flat board of wood from one end to the other. It's twenty feet long, half a foot

* See https://gettingthingsdone.com/newsletters/archive/0909.html.

deep and two feet wide. It's lying on the floor before you. You're capable of the task. You have everything you need to complete it. You could foxtrot across the board and you'd be fine. But some people raise the board. They place it 100 feet up in the air, spanning two buildings, and then they fill the alleyway below with shark-infested water. This, of course, is all happening in their mind, but it seems real. As a result, they can't cross the board. They've raised the status of the task to life or death and they hover at the edge, terrified.

Let's leave the last word on this to American sociologist Jack Mezirow. He argued that learning occurs when we change our 'frames of reference' – personal points of view or perspectives. We can change our thinking by 'elaborating existing frames of reference, by learning new frames of reference, by transforming points of view, or by transforming habits of mind' (Mezirow, 2000, p. 19). This, he argues, requires critical reflection – something this task will help you with. Only one person can be in charge of your thoughts – you. So you have to be firm and not take any nonsense.

- Catastrophe thinking becomes: 'I'm capable of performing pretty well. I'm prepared. The feedback I get will be useful.'
- Stopper thinking becomes: 'I'm learning. I'm getting better each time I hit a challenge like this. There's bound to be something I learn as a result. Mistakes are information.'
- Illogical thinking becomes: 'There's no direct connection between this and that. The past does not equal the future. Tomorrow's another day.'
- 'Not fair' thinking becomes: 'It's a straightforward enough task. I can handle it. There's a good reason for doing this that I'm not able to see.'
- Blaming thinking becomes: 'It's happened. It doesn't matter whose fault it was. The important thing is to move on and learn from it.'
- Overgeneralising becomes: 'There are a few problems I'm dealing with at the moment. Everyone has tough times and I'm no exception. But I know I'm strong enough to cope.'

Get your self-talk right, and your tendency to procrastinate will diminish.

Thoughts, plans, ideas:

26. Attitude Activity: Force Field Analysis

Sometimes we like to believe our own opinions without stress testing them. It's worth having a go at this activity to help you face the dip objectively. Force Field Analysis is a method for listing, discussing and assessing the various forces for and against a challenge you are facing. It helps you to look at the big picture by analysing all of the forces impacting on you and weighing up the pros and cons. Having identified these, you can then develop strategies to reduce the impact of the opposing forces and strengthen the supporting forces. So, if you are finding it difficult to motivate yourself towards a certain aspect of your studies, this might be one for you.

Forces that help you to achieve the challenge are called *driving forces*. These are all the reasons why you should push on through the dip. List every single benefit you can come up with: the rewards you might get for finishing, the people who'll be delighted for you, the positive feelings you'll experience. Draw up a huge energising list. Forces that work against the challenge are called *restraining forces* – the blockages and obstacles that stop you making progress.

Use the following table to chart the forces affecting you with regard to a particular challenge you're facing. Rank them by strength, listing the driving forces on the left and the restraining forces on the right. The important thing to do is to make sure the driving forces are more numerous and compelling than the restraining forces!

The Challenge

Driving forces →	Current state	← Restraining forces

You'll notice we've given you fewer lines to record your restraining forces. This is because, psychologically, you need to have a longer list of positive driving forces. This more detailed list will help you go into a challenge with a more confident attitude. Is there one thing you can do that will remove a restraining force from your list? Or is there an additional driving force you can add?

Take the action now.

27. Effort Activity: Twenty-Five Minute Sprints

There's a very famous book by Italian entrepreneur and author Francesco Cirillo called *The Pomodoro Technique*. Pomodoro is Italian for tomato. (The tomato in question is one of those novelty kitchen timers, not a real one!)

In his book, Cirillo argues that we can generate lots of energy and effort by working in short bursts, even on long tasks that we don't feel motivated to do. Think of all the tasks you've got to do that you just can't bear to begin – there might be essays to write, jumbled notes to file away or a dissertation to start.

Choose one that's hanging over your head and you just don't want to do. Make a note of it here:

. . . .

Step 1

Now for the tomato. By which we mean getting hold of either a kitchen timer or the timer on your phone. Try using the app Hold for this. It's free and blocks your phone for a specific period while you study. As you complete 'holds' – periods of distraction-free work – you earn points which give you rewards. There are a number of companies on board, so it's a compelling way of creating a focus-and-reward culture for yourself.

Next, find somewhere quiet. Arrange the things you need to begin. You're going to do a twenty-five minute sprint. It's important to tell yourself this: *twenty-five minutes – that's all.* You're allowed no distractions whatsoever in that twenty-five minutes.

Now start the timer and go!

Step 2

Congratulations! You've got that nightmare task started. All of a sudden, this job is going to seem less frightening. You'll be able to come back to it.

Some suggestions for messing around with the Pomodoro Technique:

1. **The quick sprint.** Try twenty-five minutes on, twenty-five minutes off, twenty-five minutes on. It takes one hour and fifteen minutes in total, and you can do it at a regular time each day.
2. **The serious sprint.** Try twenty-five minutes on, five minutes off, twenty-five minutes on, five minutes off, twenty-five minutes on. It takes about one hour and thirty minutes, and is a useful technique for really attacking a difficult piece of work.
3. **Try measuring tasks in sprints.** How many will it take? This way, you'll develop a sense of how you work, and you can begin picking off scary tasks more quickly and easily.
4. **Try using sprints to review work.** Suddenly you'll find yourself ahead and on top of things. It's a great feeling!

Setting Up a Quick Sprint

Preparation	Twenty-five minutes on	Twenty-five minutes off	Twenty-five minutes on
• Find somewhere quiet. • Gather everything you need. • Put phone on airplane settings. • Bring up timer, set countdown and alarm. • Tell yourself: 'Just twenty-five minutes. That's all.'	• Go! • Imagine it's an exam. • Stay intense and keep going.	• Set timer and countdown. • Enjoy yourself.	• Tell yourself: 'Just one last twenty-five minute blast. That's all.' • Put phone back on airplane settings. • Return to the task.

Remember, one quick sprint per day for a week is nearly six hours' study in total.

One serious sprint per day is nearly nine hours' study per week.

You might want to chunk down large tasks and plan a fifteen or twenty hour week to make sure they get done.

28. Effort Activity: The Five P's of Giving Up a Habit

At some point there'll be something you realise you need to stop doing. You might be skipping classes, hanging out in a certain place too often, watching too much TV or eating badly. You know the habit is damaging, but that doesn't make it any easier to stop.

The five P's work well in helping you to figure out what to expect when you finally make the change and how to get ready for it.

1. Prepare

Look ahead to a period of time when you're going to quit. Make it a week or fortnight away, no further. It has to feel like it's happening *soon*. Choose a time when you're in control of the most W's possible: when, where, what and who. In other words, a time when you've got a period of established routine allowing you to make good decisions or the potential to change your where, what and who. Put a mental flag in your calendar and repeat it to yourself: I'm quitting *then*. Draw up your list of banned behaviours and write it down.

....

....

....

....

....

2. Publicise

Raise the stakes by making your decision public. This might be in a grand way - advertising the fact to a thousand followers on social media - but it's better to let a parent, friend or partner know. Tell them, *I'm doing this thing, starting at this point*. To publicise is to make yourself accountable.

3. Pre-Make Decisions

Life is full of decisions and at the end of a long period of decision making we all experience something called decision fatigue - a decrease in the quality of our decisions. Often, by the end of the day, our minor decisions have taken up a lot of mental energy, leaving our behavioural decisions as unplanned reactions. So we crumble and return to that habit we're trying to break.

This activity allows you to anticipate some of those decisions and 'pre-make' them. Use the decision making energy you've got now to plan out your responses to future events, and make decisions in the present that represent the best possible future you. First, consider these questions:

* What kind of student/person do you want to be?
* What qualities do you want to have?
* What's important to you?
* What do you want other people to say about you?
* What ideals do you want your strong, confident decisions to be based on?

Scribble down some notes and bear them in mind as you put yourself into some difficult scenarios. Some of them happen to everybody, and we've included them in the table that follows. Others might be specific to your situation, so there's a blank space on page 139 for you to add your own scenarios.

Scenario	Pre-made decision
You plan on doing some important research, but your internet connection is down ...	....
You set aside some time to catch up on some crucial work, but a friend arrives and wants to chat ...	....
You have important tasks you want to get finished, but there is something great on TV/social media/the internet ...	....
A friend asks you to skip a seminar with them ...	....
You've got a couple of hours' work ahead of you to finish a gruelling task, but the weather is beautiful outside ...	....

Use this space to record other challenges you know you're going to face, and the decisions that will go with them:

You might not always make choices that fill you with pride, but pre-making good decisions makes them more likely to happen!

4. Proxy

A proxy is a replacement for the activity you want to stop. One friend who ate badly every lunchtime, because of the calorific canteen food his workplace provided, subscribed to Graze and ate his way through four little snack boxes every day instead. Willpower alone will not get you through. You'll need some sort of crutch – the metaphorical nicotine patch that replaces whatever you usually do.

5. Persist

It isn't all smooth sailing, and the desire to return to the old habit doesn't decrease with each new day. There seem to be spikes. Day two is harder than day one. At a point two weeks into your new habit, the old one comes back to attack you again. Three weeks in, with a decent run of success, things tend to feel much better and get easier. Watch out for the mind playing tricks, though – looking for reasons to slacken off or adjust.

29. Effort Activity: The Three R's of a New Habit

Stanford University has a Behaviour Design Lab. Here, academics study how interactive technology is changing our habits. Its founder and director, Dr B. J. Fogg, is studying how mobile phone technology – apps and so on – can develop habit formation.

Effort is also a habit. The level of effort you put into your studies is a result of your habits. Some people have got the effort habit, some people haven't. The argument goes that there are three elements to habit formation, often referred to as the three R's:

1. **The reminder.** This could be a feeling, a place or a time of day – it's your body or brain giving you a trigger that initiates the behaviour. That behaviour might be getting some chocolate, going home early or putting away the work you know you should be completing.
2. **The routine**. This is the behaviour itself. Going to the canteen and buying the chocolate or taking the bus home instead of staying on to do some studying. Often people will feel a twinge of guilt during the routine but do it anyway.
3. **The reward.** This is the good feeling you get – the benefit you gain from engaging in the behaviour. It might not last long but it's a tempting prospect.

If you haven't currently got into the effort habit, how can you go about changing? You can use the three R's in your favour, and use a new reminder to trigger a new habit, a new routine to go through and, best of all, a new reward to give yourself.

Reminder:

. . . .

. . . .

. . . .

Routine:

. . . .

. . . .

. . . .

Reward:

. . . .

. . . .

. . . .

Remember, when you plan a new habit, never use the negative language associated with breaking habits; instead use positive language. Try: 'From Monday, I'm going to start working harder.'

Allow yourself slips and mistakes, and build in opportunities to take a break. Try: 'From Monday to Thursday, I'm going to really go for it. We'll see how Friday goes when I get there ...' or, 'On the days when I have to be in early, I'm going to stay and work until 3pm. On other days, I'll just see how I feel ...' If you have a slip-up, assess it calmly and then return to the habit. A single mistake doesn't invalidate what you're doing – there's no need to give everything up.

30. Attitude Activity: The First Aid Kit: Sleep, Diet and Exercise

Even the best prepared student can have moments of personal crisis. Most colleges and universities have a counselling service for students struggling with their mental health, although your GP should always be your first port of call for serious mental health problems.

The following activities are designed to help as a quick reminder of some basic steps you can take to keep your operating system functioning on top form. You will have probably come across some of them before, but quite often these simple acts can make a big difference.

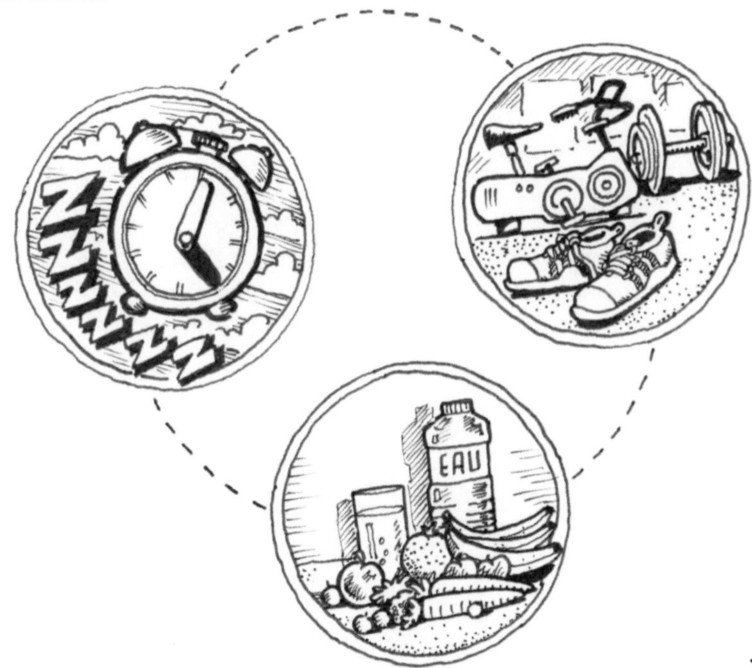

Going Dark and Sleep

What do you use as an alarm clock? Nowadays, the answer is invariably 'my phone'. The blue-green light of late-night screen use, as most of us know, encourages melatonin production in the brain and 'tricks' us into thinking it's daytime. Sleep becomes elusive, levels of concentration drop and the ability to control difficult or damaging emotions falls away pretty steeply.

When you're feeling overwhelmed, consider trying a digital detox or setting all your social media feeds to 'Back in a month!' Many students find that this has a huge impact on how they feel. If you can't face leaving social media for a period of time, at least try not to use your phone or laptop for an hour before you go to bed. Keep it up for a week and see how you feel.

Caffeine, Protein and Sleep

Just like a digital detox before bed, it's worth considering the caffeine levels in energy drinks and soft drinks. Most students are pretty clued up on sugar content but we've come across a significant number of students who think diet drinks are free from everything and therefore a safe bet for continuous consumption.

There are a whole host of online resources regularly updated about caffeine in soft drinks, giving you milligrams per 100ml of liquid (watch out for American sites, as drinks have higher levels in the US). Most experts suggest avoiding consuming any caffeinated drinks after 2pm.

Protein-rich foods give an energy boost before bed whereas carbs promote drowsiness. We've found that super-healthy gym types know their low-carb diet pretty well but make the mistake of hoovering up protein-heavy suppers which prevent good sleep.

Keeping a simple diary like the one on the next page can help you to identify any patterns.

Sleep diary				
Date:				
Bedtime:	Wake time:	Sleep duration:	No. of times awake:	Sleep quality:
Caffeine intake and time taken	**Alcohol intake and time taken**	**Food/drink intake and time taken**	**How are you feeling?**	**Medications**
....	....	....	....	....
....	....	....	....	....
....	....	....	....	....
....	....	....	....	....
....	....	....	....	....
....	....	....	....	....
....	....	....	....	....
....	....	....	....	....

Exercise

For runners, swimmers and gym-goers this is an easy one. For the rest of us, there's always walking. There's plenty of research that suggests just twenty minutes of walking every day can have a genuine impact on our well-being.

We've experimented with helping students with walking for mindfulness or therapy in the past, and this is one of our favourite walking activities.

MINDFULL or MINDFUL?

Choose a destination that is about a twenty minute walk away.

Walk there. While you walk, you can only think positive thoughts. The topics are: things I am good at, things I am thankful for. Nothing else can enter your mind. If you find your mind wandering, gently bring it back and keep focusing on these two topics. When you arrive, or as you go, record your thoughts or list them quickly on a notepad.

Now return to where you set out. While you walk back, you're allowed to address any problems you're facing. But here's the crucial point –

the topic is: things I can do to solve my problems. Again, the key is to be strong with yourself. This is the only thing you can think about, and if your thoughts deviate, bring them back as soon as you realise what's happened. When you arrive back, take a few minutes alone and make a note of your thoughts and ideas.

Some people repeat this activity a couple of times a month to help them refocus. One person we know has the top of a hill as their destination - they say that walking down it helps to relax them after the hard slog of getting to the top, and they always come up with actions they can take to solve problems on the way down.

There's also mindful walking to consider. We've read a whole host of advice on this and distilled it into our version, in which students take a short, daily walk during May and June. Choose a circuit that takes about twenty minutes to complete. Your aim is to focus on (1) the quality of your breath as you walk and (2) broadening your attention - that is, actively looking at the world around you as you go.

Don't worry if you find your attention wandering. This is perfectly normal. All you have to do is gently and non-judgementally return your attention to the breath and to the activity of watching the world around you; of being an objective observer rather than an introspective tangle of stress.

You'll be amazed by what you start to notice, even if you've walked the route hundreds of times before!

Conclusion

Ten Final Thoughts

You're likely to have experienced an education system built on the notion that past performance equals future performance. Mike Treadaway from FFT Education Datalab describes it like this in his 2015 paper: 'Take a child's attainment at age 7, look up the average attainment for children at the same level by age 11 and draw a straight line between the two assuming that linear progress will be made in each of the four intervening years.'

But Treadaway challenges the past-equals-future model. He's got reservations about whether learners follow this neat upward trajectory. Some do, he finds, but very, very few. 'By reviewing the data,' Treadaway notes, 'we find that only 9% of pupils take the expected pathways through Key Stage Two, Key Stage Three and Key Stage Four Levels.' Fewer than one in ten students follow the past-equals-future line that most colleges use to anticipate and measure progress. Performance at point A (wherever you choose that to be) doesn't guarantee performance at point B.

This is good news for all of us trying to learn something new. Whatever we've done in the past has little or no bearing on what we can achieve now. Instead, we believe there are five non-cognitive skill areas that play a key role in determining our success, and these five elements – having a vision, making a habit of effort, building effective systems, engaging in high stakes practice and having the correct attitude – can be practised and learned.

On Vision

1 Having a clear sense of what success looks like is central – it's something we've seen over and over again in successful students. But visions don't have to be jobs or careers. Build flexibility into your goals by concentrating on purpose and problem: what am I here to do with my life? How do I want to leave the world a better place? What needs to be accomplished? What makes me feel alive and positive and purposeful? Increasing self-knowledge, even if it's a sense of 'what makes me tick', 'what I like doing' or 'what fascinates me', builds vision.

2 Long-term goals are magnetic, but we've spoken to students who are adept at making short-term goals magnetic too. If you can't think about what life will be like in a year's time, try monthly or fortnightly goal setting (What would the perfect project submission look like? What actions can I take in the next three weeks to make that outcome more likely?) and reward yourself for hitting those milestones.

On Effort

3 Effort is the product of routine and habit. We've been lucky enough to see lots of students change their habits. Very small, sustained improvements quickly beat huge revolutions in effort that can't be sustained. One thing that successful students have taught us is that, as we establish new habits, self-sabotage is the enemy. The five glitches come from ourselves. Study is about recognising our potential weaknesses and mastering ourselves as much as mastering our subjects.

4 Successful learners have often established for themselves a set of leading indicators that they work on all the time. If you can devise a set of leading indicator study habits for yourself, you can track your progress against them.

On Systems

5 If there is one strategy we've learned from speaking to super-organised learners, it's to snack rather than binge. Little and

often beats cramming hands down. That means subdividing tasks into component parts – in other words, chunking them. Chunking tasks makes them far less scary and it makes self-assessment of progress easier.

6 We've finally figured out what high systems students have known for a long time – that if you assign the right kind of task to the right time of day, you can get it done much more quickly. They get more done in less time because they batch similar tasks together, or block out time for deep work, or remove tasks that aren't having an impact on their learning.

On Practice

7 In the past it was your teachers who adjusted challenge in class, moving you and your fellow pupils out of comfort, relaxation or even boredom into more uncertain territory. But when you're working alone, you are the one who has to do this. The majority of the unhappy and underperforming students we've talked to had designed comfortable, non-challenging practice routines that left them bored and distracted.

8 Effective practice is high stakes and uncomfortable. Study is intellectual combat. It should feel hard.

On Attitude

9 The successful students we've talked to wanted to succeed more than they feared failure. For them, mistakes were crucial – failure was a necessary part of learning. We weren't always like that as learners; our tendency was to hide our inability, refuse help, give up. As students, we need to fail and collect feedback – it gives us powerful information with which to work.

10 All learners experience setbacks and lousy learning experiences – but some have developed a set of psychological tricks, tools and tactics to get them through. They have learned to review the benefits of tough times and to expect the rocky road.

The successful student mindset is the result of a large number of interconnected qualities. But much of our mindset is developed unconsciously through parenting, schooling or the influence of peers. A neat experiment run by Barry Zimmerman at New York university in the early 1980s demonstrates this well. Zimmerman and Ringle (1981) gave students an impossible challenge (untangling a knot of wires) and an adult to model the process of problem solving before giving them a go too. One group got a pessimistic adult: 'I don't think I can separate these wires,' they said after a period of trying. 'I've tried many different ways and nothing seems to work.' The other group got an optimistic adult who, experiencing struggle, said things like, 'I'm sure I can separate these wires; I just have to keep trying different ways and then I'll find the right one.'

Of course, students in this second group (despite being no more successful than the others) reported higher levels of confidence and positivity and, as a result, persisted for longer. They had a better mindset.

Much of our personal mindset has been formed through what Albert Bandura (1997) calls 'vicarious experiences', like the one illustrated above. If we are to really reach our potential, we have to first recognise our current mindset and the reasons for its existence. We can then, if necessary, go about changing it, one small step at a time.

Hopefully this short handbook has given you some starting points.

References

Allan, D. (2015). *Getting Things Done: The Art of Stress-Free Productivity*, new edn (London: Piatkus).

Aristotle (2009). *The Nicomachean Ethics*, ed. L. Brown, tr. D. Ross (Oxford: Oxford University Press).

Bandura, A. (1997). *Self-Efficacy: The Exercise of Control* (New York: Freeman).

Belsky, S. (2010). *Making Ideas Happen: Overcoming the Obstacles Between Vision and Reality* (London: Penguin).

Brock, T. (2016). How to be successful, according to Jimmy Kimmel, Gary Vaynerchuk and Charlie Brock. *Business Journals* (5 October). Available at: https://www.bizjournals.com/bizjournals/how-to/growth-strategies/2016/10/how-to-be-successful-according-to-jimmy-kimmel.html.

Bull, S. (2006). *The Game Plan: Your Guide to Mental Toughness at Work* (Chichester: Capstone Publishing).

Canfield, J. (2005). *The Success Principles: How to Get from Where You Are to Where You Want to Be* (London: HarperCollins).

Carson, R. (1965). *The Sense of Wonder* (New York: Harper & Row).

Cirillo, F. (2017). *The Pomodoro Technique: Do More and Have Fun with Time Management* (London: Ebury Publishing).

Collins, D. and MacNamara, A. (2012). The rocky road to the top: why talent needs trauma. *Sports Medicine* 42(11): 907–914.

Collins, J. (2001). *Good to Great* (London: Random House Business).

Cooper, C., Sullivan, A. and Shulman, J. (1978). *Making It in College: Strategies for Studying and Learning* (East Lansing, MI: Michigan State University).

Covey, S. R. (1989). *The 7 Habits of Highly Effective People* (London: Simon & Schuster).

Coyle, D. (2009). *The Talent Code: Greatness Isn't Born. It's Grown. Here's How* (New York: Bantam).

Coyle, D. (2012). *The Little Book of Talent* (London: Random House).

Csikszentmihalyi, M. (1997). *Finding Flow: The Psychology of Discovery and Invention* (New York: Harper Perennial).

Csikszentmihalyi, M. (2003). *Good Business: Leadership, Flow and the Making of Meaning* (New York: Penguin).

Dalio, R. (2017). *Principles* (New York: Simon & Schuster).

Duckworth, A. L. (2016). *Grit: The Power of Passion and Perseverance* (London: Penguin Random House).

Dunlosky, J., Rawson, K. A., Marsh, E. J., Nathan, M. J. and Willingham, D. T. (2013). Improving students' learning with effective learning techniques: promising directions from cognitive and educational psychology. *Psychological Science in the Public Interest* 14(1): 4 –58.

Ellis, A. (1957). Rational psychotherapy and individual psychology. *Journal of Individual Psychology* 13: 38–44.

Ellis, A. (1998). *How to Stubbornly Refuse to Make Yourself Miserable About Anything (Yes, Anything!)* (New York: Citadel Press).

Emmons, R. A. and McCullough, M. E. (2003). Counting blessings versus burdens: an experimental investigation of gratitude and subjective well-being in daily life. *Journal of Personality and Social Psychology* 84(2): 377–389.

Ericsson, K. A. and Pool, R. (2016). *Peak: Secrets from the New Science of Expertise* (Boston, MA: Houghton Mifflin Harcourt).

Ferriss, T. (2007). *The 4-Hour Work Week: Escape the 9–5, Live Anywhere and Join the New Rich* (New York: Crown).

Ferriss, T. (2017a). Managing Procrastination, Predicting the Future, and Finding Happiness – Tim Urban (#283). *The Tim Ferriss Show* (3 November) [audio interview with Tim Urban]. Available at: https://tim.blog/2017/11/30/managing-procrastination-predicting-the-future-and-finding-happiness/.

Ferriss, T. (2017b). *Tribe of Mentors: Short Life Advice from the Best in the World* (London: Vermilion).

Fiore, N. (2007). *The Now Habit: A Strategic Program for Overcoming Procrastination and Enjoying Guilt-Free Play* (New York: Tarcher Perigee).

Fitts, P. M. and Posner, M. I. (1967). *Human Performance* (Belmont, CA: Brooks/Cole).

Geirland, J. (1996). Go with the flow [interview with Mihaly Csikszentmihalyi]. *Wired* (4 September). Available at: https://www.wired.com/1996/09/czik/.

Gilbert, I. (2014). *Independent Thinking* (Carmarthen: Independent Thinking Press).

Gladwell, M. (2008). *Outliers: The Story of Success* (New York: Little, Brown and Company).

Godin, S. (2007). *The Dip: The Extraordinary Benefits of Knowing When to Quit (and When to Stick)* (London: Piatkus).

Haring, N. G., Lovitt, T. C., Eaton, M. D. and Hansen, C. L. (1978). *The Fourth R: Research in the Classroom* (Columbus, OH: Merrill).

Kleon, A. (2014). *Show Your Work! 10 Things Nobody Told You About Getting Discovered* (New York: Algonquin Books).

Kotler, S. (2014). *The Rise of the Superman: Decoding the Science of Ultimate Human Performance* (London: Quercus).

Kübler-Ross, E. (1969). *On Death and Dying* (London: Routledge).

Leitner, S. (2011). *So lernt man lernen* (How We Learn) (Hamburg: Nikol Verlagsgesellschaft mbH).

McChesney, C., Covey, S. and Huling, J. (2012). *The 4 Disciplines of Execution: Achieving Your Wildly Important Goals* (New York: Simon & Schuster).

McLeod, S. A. (2017). Kolb – learning styles. *Simply Psychology*. Available at: https://www.simplypsychology.org/learning-kolb.html.

Martin, A. (2010). *Building Classroom Success: Eliminating Academic Fear and Failure* (London: Continuum).

Maslow, A. H. (2000). *The Maslow Business Reader*, ed. D. C. Stephens (New York: John Wiley & Sons).

Maxwell, J. (2012). *Failing Forward: Turning Mistakes into Stepping Stones for Success* (Nashville, TN: Thomas Nelson Publishing).

Mezirow, J. (2000). Learning to think like an adult: core concepts of transformation theory. In Mezirow, J. (ed), *Learning as Transformation: Critical Perspectives on a Theory in*

Progress (San Francisco, CA: Jossey-Bass), pp. 3–34.

Ottati, V., Price, E. D., Wilson, C. and Sumaktoyo, N. (2015). When self-perceptions of expertise increase closed-minded cognition: the earned dogmatism effect. *Journal of Experimental Social Psychology* 61: 131–138. Available at: https://www.sciencedirect.com/science/article/pii/S0022103115001006.

Owen, J. (2015). *The Mindset of Success: Accelerate Your Career from Good Manager to Great Leader* (London: Kogan Page).

Popova, M. (2011). Scott Belsky on how to avoid idea plateaus. *Brain Pickings* (18 March). Available at: https://www.brainpickings.org/2011/03/18/scott-belsky-idea-plateaus/.

Price, A. and Price, D. (2011). *Psychology of Success: A Practical Guide* (London: Icon Books).

Reiss, S. (2000). *Who Am I? The 16 Basic Desires That Motivate Our Actions and Define Our Personalities* (New York: Tarcher/Putnum).

Schank, R. C., Lyras, D. and Soloway, E. (2010). *The Future of Decision Making: How Revolutionary Software Can Improve the Ability to Decide* (New York: Palgrave Macmillan).

Seelig, T. (2012). *inGenius: A Crash Course on Creativity* (London: Hay House).

Sinek, S. (2009). *Start With Why: How Great Leaders Inspire Everyone to Take Action* (London Penguin Random House).

Suzuki, S. (2005). *Zen Mind, Beginner's Mind*, new edn (Boston, MA: Shambhala Publications).

Treadaway, M. (2015). Why measuring pupil progress involves more than taking a straight line. *Education Datalab* (5 March). Available at: https://educationdatalab.org.uk/2015/03/why-measuring-pupil-progress-involves-morethan-taking-a-straight-line/.

Troyat, H. (2001 [1967]). *Tolstoy*, tr. N. Amphoux (New York: Double Day/Grove Press).

von Oech, R. (1992). *A Whack on the Side of the Head: How You Can Be More Creative* (New York: Warner Books).

Woodward, A. (2018). No sweat: how can marathon runners avoid hitting 'the wall'? *New Scientist* (10 January). Available at: https://www.newscientist.com/article/mg23731600-600-can-you-avoid-hitting-the-wall/.

Wulf, G. (2007). *Attention and Motor Skill Learning* (Champaign, IL: Human Kinetics).

Zimmerman, B. J. and Ringle, J. (1981). Effects of model persistence and statements of confidence on children's efficacy and problem solving. *Journal of Educational Psychology* 73(4): 485–493.